D1111443

UNREACHABLE

UNREACHABLE

A TRUE STORY

DARRELL TUNNINGLEY

Sovereign World

Sovereign World Ltd
PO Box 784
Ellel
Lancaster
LA1 9DA
United Kingdom

www.sovereignworld.com

ISBN: 978 1 85240 589 2

The publishers aim to produce books which will help to extend and build up
the Kingdom of God. We do not necessarily agree with every view expressed
by the authors, or with every interpretation of Scripture expressed. We expect
readers to make their own judgment in the light of their understanding of
God's Word and in an attitude of Christian love and fellowship.

Typeset by The Book Design Company
Printed in the United Kingdom

CONTENTS

I would like to dedicate this book to my beautiful wife Rebekah, for being with me every step of the journey. And to our fantastic children, Benjamin and Lydia.

ACKNOWLEDGEMENTS

Firstly to Jesus, for saving a sinner like me. He's my everything. He's my lifeline, He's my strength, I couldn't live without Him, and everything I do is through Him and for Him. My life wouldn't be the way it is if He wasn't exactly who He said He was.

To Rita Nightingale and Joyce Mulvee for investing their time and discipling me in prison.

To Malcolm Bailey who first steered me towards ministry; he has gone to be with Jesus before seeing this book come to life.

To my parents, for sticking with me through the bad and good.

To my pastor, Mark Finch, for stepping out in faith with me and guiding me through the last eleven years.

To my family at Hope Corner Community Church, who have walked with me where God has taken me.

To Paul Stanier and all the team at Sovereign World for being part of this journey and catching the vision of what God wants to do through this project.

And finally to Sheila Jacobs – her hard work and editing skills have turned my scribbles into a great book.

FOREWORD

I walked into the head teacher's office wondering why the senior leadership of the school had summoned me. As the door opened, I became immediately aware of the penetrating gaze from the head and deputy head. In the deputy head's hand was a substantial report concerning someone I had recently invited to join our team.

This was the same bold leadership that had invited me into their school two years earlier to help support a substantial minority of vulnerable young people who were not coping with the normal routine that education demands. The pressures of life outside school were crowding out their ability to learn, leading to times of disruption and even, in some cases, judicial involvement.

As the leader of a newly planted church in Runcorn, I felt that the opportunity to minister into this large comprehensive school was a major door that God had opened up to us. The school leadership had given me and my small team of volunteers the freedom to support these young people not only practically, but also in a spiritual capacity. They'd also provided us with an area of the school that was for our exclusive use.

In the first two years of this ministry, we had witnessed some incredible breakthroughs with many teenagers, who had also begun to fill our church services week by week. Yet there was still a "hardcore" element that, on the face of it, seemed unreachable. These were young people who had become dependent on drugs and violence to survive day by day. It would have been very simple to just dismiss this group, particularly as they seemed to be so abusive towards us, but God kept speaking to us about them. One of the barriers we were facing was the fact that none of us had any experience of dealing with drug issues.

At about this time, I was invited to the performance of a passion play at a prison in Rochdale. What intrigued me was the fact that the actors were all inmates who had become Christians while serving their sentences.

After the performance, I met the actors, one of whom was a young man called Darrell Tunningley. He had become a Christian through an Alpha course that had taken place in prison. He outlined his background to me, which included the world of drugs and violence. He also told me how, in partnership with a friend, they had developed a very successful drugs awareness programme that had made a profound difference to many in that prison. Travelling home that night, I knew God was speaking to me about Darrell becoming one of the major keys that would help unlock the lives of the young people in Runcorn. Even though this was the case, I didn't anticipate the obstacles that would need to be faced in order for Darrell to minister into a school situation.

The biggest of those obstacles was this report the deputy head teacher was holding in his hand as I walked into the office. It had come from the Probation Service and gave every detail of a young man fresh out of prison who was about to become part of our team.

The head teacher greeted me in a polite but firm voice with the question, "Do you know what is in this report?"

"Yes," I said. "It recommends that you should not allow Darrell to work in this school."

In that moment I realized that the future of Darrell's ministry to young people not only in that school but in the entire area was in the balance. As I prayed about what to say next, another question came at me: "Do you believe he has really changed?"

Before she had barely finished, I replied, "Yes, he certainly has, and he will help make a positive difference to the students here."

The statement that they made next was nothing short of the embodiment of a miracle second only to Darrell's own conversion captured in this book. "In that case, on your recommendation we invite Darrell to work with you in this school."

It didn't take long for that decision to be vindicated, with Darrell's work making an impact not only on young people's lives, but also on the lives of parents, teachers, professionals and even government officials.

If you think the age of miracles is over, think again. Darrell's story will give you an appetite to see the impossible made possible.

Mark B.J. Finch
Senior Minister
Hope Corner Community Church, Runcorn

INTRODUCTION

If you have picked up this book because you feel that you are so messed up that you are beyond fixing, that you have gone too far the wrong way to ever be given a second chance, then I pray that the story you are about to read will show you that nobody is beyond God's forgiveness.

If you have picked up this book because you look at the lost in this world and wonder how "little old you" could possibly reach out to them, then I pray that you realize the great truth that God can use anyone – if they just follow where He leads.

Darrell Tunningley
August 2011

CHAPTER 1

Early Days

One day, as I was sifting through old papers in the loft, I came across my old school reports. As I sat back and started to read, I realized they all had one thing in common. They all said, "could do better" or "not achieving your full potential". How right they were! My life was one of continual ups and downs; it was like a roller coaster that was about to go off the rails. But then something happened that would change that ride from out-of-control fear and anger to one of excitement and surprise.

Growing up in Knottingley, West Yorkshire, I was into all kinds of trouble – drinking, taking drugs and stealing cars. I would love to say that I didn't start off bad, but if I'm honest I always seemed to be very good at lies and deceit. I can't have been more than nine or ten years old when I stole a gold chain from my mum's jewellery box. I got caught because I tried to sell it to one of her friends, saying I had found it. But she recognized it as my mum's, and told her.

Back then, I remember looking around at my mates who always seemed to have the best trainers, clothes and money. My mum and dad worked hard, but money was always tight. So I came to the conclusion that the easiest way to get the things I wanted was to steal them.

I was always getting into trouble, then trying to lie my way out of it. A lot of the time it worked, so I kept on getting better and better at it. A craze in those days was nicking car badges from expensive cars such as Mercedes and Porsches. Me and my friends would collect and trade these badges as if they were comic books. After a while we moved on to shoplifting. The more I stole, the more my confidence grew. It's scary how quickly you can go from stealing Mars bars to cars! We would dare each other to steal bigger and more expensive things, and we always seemed to get away with it.

I just seemed to have something pulling me to do the things that were wrong – breaking into buildings such as schools and offices just to trash them and gain some status because everyone knew I had done it. I can't even blame peer pressure, because a lot of the time I was the ringleader!

When my mates were starting to smoke, I went and got some cigarettes on my own so I could practise and then show off in front of them all. I knew I didn't like smoking because when I was nine I had nicked one of my mum's cigarettes while she was out at the shops. I remember taking one drag on it and throwing up in the kitchen sink! But here I was smoking away to impress my mates. And before I knew it, I was addicted to nicotine.

To most people, I suppose everything about me seemed pretty normal and, on the surface, it was for a while. I was doing OK at school, good at sports, nothing out of the ordinary … but there was always this self-destructive time bomb just waiting to go off.

My interest in drugs started early with smoking weed (cannabis) and sniffing solvents. I would even steal paint thinners from the woodwork shop to get off my face between lessons – anything to get away from reality for a while. By the time I was eleven or twelve, every Friday and Saturday night would be about getting the strongest drink I could for the lowest price, and getting so drunk I couldn't walk. Then I would try to sober up enough to hide it when I got home. If I wasn't drinking, I was smoking weed, or sniffing solvents or petrol.

I was an angry young man, but didn't really know what I was angry about. I was rebelling, but wasn't sure what I was rebelling against. There were arguments at home, but these seemed to be the norm; I'd just stay out as often and for as long as I possibly could.

There were periods where things were good. I made a new group of friends and joined the Army Cadets, thriving under the structure and discipline. I absolutely loved it. When I was coming towards the end of school, I wanted to join the army. My dad refused point-blank to sign the papers and we ended up in a fight over it. I can understand now why they didn't want me to join, but it made me even more rebellious – if I couldn't do what I wanted, then I was determined to wreck everything.

The lesson I learned pretty early on was that when I was stoned or drunk, then all these problems in my teenage life just faded away for a while; there was no pressure and I could be in control. Or so I thought.

While all this was going on, I was also living a seemingly normal life. It was as if there was a parallel universe that was running alongside the other, rebellious, life I was living. I was playing Rugby League for my local side and school, and I was really into Tae Kwon Do. At fifteen, I was training twice a week, fighting in competitions and teaching women's self-defence classes. I was good; I loved the meditation that accompanied the discipline, and the self-control. It always seemed to calm the demons and confusion in my mind. Having a sense of purpose and worth helped to keep away the destructive side of my nature for a while.

The problem was that keeping these two separate lives going was tearing me apart. My life always felt off balance, as though there was something missing or there had to be something more. It sounds a bit bigheaded, but I felt as if I was meant for greater things. I was always a little too clever for my own good; lying and deception seemed to come pretty easily to me, and for the most part I was smart enough not to get caught. I look at young people now, and I don't need to ask the question "Why do you use drugs?" They use for the same reasons I did. They do it to escape it all – whatever "it all" is; the pressures of life, trouble at home, absent fathers. Escaping even for a short while is better than having to face it.

I managed to make it through high school with no major dramas. My exam results were not great, but good enough to get me on the college course I was interested in, and for a short time things seemed to be OK. I was studying sports science at Wakefield College, and my rugby career seemed to be heading in the right direction. I was playing for Huddersfield Giants and later for Featherstone Rovers. Playing at a professional level meant training almost every day. I was keeping busy, staying out of trouble and becoming extremely fit and strong.

I thought that rugby could be my ticket out, an escape, but injury and my own bad decisions would put an end to my rugby career. Apart from a serious injury to my knee, I also skipped a drugs test. Failing to provide a sample meant being banned – but providing a positive would have got me banned anyway. So at that point, Rugby League wasn't an option any more. I packed in college as well.

I'd had my life kind of planned out and had thought I knew where it was going, but now everything felt like it was going into a free fall. Little did I know at the time that a few wrong decisions and a strange desire to self-destruct would mean that the world of drugs and violence would become my new career.

CHAPTER 2

SLIDING DOWN

Because I would never "achieve my full potential" in rugby, just as the teachers had predicted, the lure of drugs began to pull me further and further in. I felt as though everything in my life was heading the wrong way; nothing I tried worked or went right. The more setbacks that I experienced, the angrier I became. So I started going to illegal raves and found a new way of escaping my reality. Ecstasy and amphetamine were my new drugs of choice, and I found that all my problems disappeared when they were in control. But while the drugs covered over all my feelings for a while, when the effects wore off they just became another of the problems I had to deal with. It became a cycle of destruction.

Unfortunately it wasn't just the drugs that became addictive; it was the whole lifestyle that came with it. Everyone at a rave becomes your family. Everyone was "loved up" on ecstasy, speed and cocaine, out for a great time and accepting anyone and everyone, no matter who they were. Everyone on the rave scene lived for the weekend so they could do it all over again.

My friends and I had our own mixing decks and would have our own raves wherever and whenever we could. The problem was, we wouldn't just get "pilled-up" at the weekends – it began to spread into the weekdays as well. Before I knew it, I was pilled-up pretty much every day, going on huge benders, then taking days to recover.

This amount of drug use needed money, and we soon discovered that the easiest way to get money was to become dealers, taking the profits to fund our own use. This is how things stayed for a while.

The main club we would go to was in Doncaster; every Saturday night we would follow the same routine. We would meet up at a mate's flat and start doing lines of cocaine or amphetamine with "happy hardcore" and "techno" tunes banging out. Around 10 p.m. we would start taking ecstasy, before heading off to the rave. I was about sixteen by this point and most of my mates were older than me, which helped when getting into clubs. We knew most of the door staff, so taking drugs in was usually just a quick £50 in their pocket and in you went.

It was during one of these "ordinary" Saturday nights that something happened to one of my mates that would change his life for ever. Andy had been taking ecstasy for a couple of years, but this night things would go drastically wrong for him. We had all taken pills and were sitting around listening to music before going out, when Andy started to convulse. At first we thought he was messing about, but it was soon obvious he wasn't. We picked him up and took him into the bathroom to stick him under a cold shower. That didn't help, so we dialled 999. An ambulance arrived, Andy was taken away, and the rest of us cleared off to the rave. We later found out that Andy had had an epileptic fit triggered by the ecstasy. He would be on medication for epilepsy for the rest of his life.

More often than not raves were trouble-free, because when you are "loved up" on ecstasy, fighting is the last thing on your mind. But every so often violence would creep in. At the club in Doncaster, they used to have a big double-decker bus outside that had been turned into a chill-out area, somewhere to cool down and re-hydrate. You were lucky if you could get a seat because it was also where everyone went to "cop off" with the opposite sex! Once, when I was sitting on the bus with a couple of mates, catching my breath and having a drink after a few hours' dancing, a huge guy with massive dreadlocks came walking over and slammed a machete down on the table in front of me. Before I could say anything or even react, he just said, "Sorry, wrong person", and walked off. I looked at my mates and we laughed, and just got on with our night.

The problem for people who use stimulant drugs such as ecstasy and amphetamine is the comedown; as the drugs wear off, you feel horrible. It's like a really bad hangover, but you can't sleep or eat until the drugs have really worn off. If you've been out at a rave from midnight till ten in the morning, then all you want to do is get your head down – but you can't, because of the amount of stimulants in your system.

Then someone offered me a solution. Heroin! If you smoked a downer drug to counter the stimulants, then you could chill out and sleep after your night of raving. It was a quick-fix answer to me, and I didn't think twice. That was my biggest mistake. Using heroin would take my life down a very dark and slippery road.

It happened after a long night of clubbing. The stimulant drugs were wearing off and we had all gone back to Nick's house to come down. Nick had already scored some heroin; I watched him smoke a few lines and instantly start to chill out. I couldn't resist it.

"Pass us a few lines, Nick."

"OK." He handed me the foil, I put the tooter (like a small tube made of tin foil) in my mouth, and smoked my first line. To begin with it tasted horrible, but as the heroin kicked in I didn't care. This was something new, a high like I'd never felt before. The drug washed over me and brought me down from the stimulant drugs in my system.

When I first started to use heroin I truly believed that I would stay in control, and that the drug would never control me. How wrong I was! My relationship with my family was already in a mess because of my drug use and lifestyle choices. I would simply go missing for days and weeks without them knowing where I was or what I was doing. It was usually because I was on a bender with the drugs or locked up for one crime or another, usually managing to get bail and allowed back on the streets.·

My parents, at the time, knew very little about drug use. I guess all they could see was the child they'd known slipping away from them little by little. As the drugs gained a stronger hold, it caused the gap between my family and me to grow wider and wider. Looking back, I think they must have felt powerless; not knowing the best way to deal with what was happening, or understanding why it was happening at all.

As well as selling drugs, we were committing more and more crimes as well – robberies, car theft, commercial burglaries to name just a few. More often than not, it wasn't just planned crimes. I would take amazingly stupid risks and not care about the consequences. There was one time that I was in Selby, South Yorkshire to do a deal. I ended up getting arrested by South Yorkshire police because I had used a stolen car to travel there. I was held until the early hours and eventually let go but I was left with no way to get back to West Yorkshire. As I was walking down the road I came across a truck yard. I noticed there was a wagon with no trailer, left unattended with its engine running. I glanced around, nobody about.

"Well," I said to myself, "it's easier than trying to nick a car with no tools!" So I jumped in the cab and drove it all the way back home, having never driven a wagon before. I dumped it down a side street.

I seemed to be able to stay one step ahead of the law most of the time, but as my drug use increased, so did the risks. Once, I was at a huge rave near Sheffield. It had been advertised as the biggest drug-free rave ever; "Sure," I thought, "it might be the biggest, but no way is it going to be drug-free!" Me and my friends headed there with drugs for our own personal use, and plenty to sell.

The night was going well and it only went wrong because I got sloppy. I went into the toilets and did some cocaine. I was so out of it that I didn't realize there was coke all over my nose. Police were everywhere, and as soon as I came out they saw me and arrested me for possession.

There were so many people at this "drug-free" rave getting arrested that they were just marching us all out and sticking us in vans. Just as I had been put in the van, troubled kicked off nearby and the officers who were with me ran to assist. I couldn't believe my luck; I hadn't been cuffed, and I had a mix of ecstasy, amphetamine and cocaine in a bag in my sock! My mind had been spinning about how to get rid of the drugs, so I quickly stuffed them down a gap in the seat. There were a few of us in the van and they had been ferrying people back to the station all night, so I knew they couldn't tie the drugs to me. I was right. I was released after a couple of hours.

Time after time I continued to escape by the skin of my teeth. I was arrested for an assault. When the police picked me up for it on the street, I had just collected some stolen credit cards and was taking them to be used. Usually when you get picked up you are booked and searched at the station, but when we got there the holding cells were full and the desk sergeant said, "Just stick him in that interview room for now." I couldn't believe it. As soon as I was alone I made a little rip in the material underneath the chair and slid the cards in. Were they ever found? I don't know!

It wasn't just risks where the police were involved, either. My mate Mick had set up a meeting with a guy in Hull about a large amount of drugs. The problem was, Mick had been locked up the night before. We wanted the meet to still take place, so I took Mick's car and drove over to see the guy. When I got there, he was waiting on the street so I pulled up to talk to him. I wound down the window and was explaining why it was me meeting him and not Mick when I heard a loud bang. Everything happened so fast. He fell on the ground, my headrest exploded and the back window smashed. Someone had shot at us, but to this day I don't know whether the target was him or me. Being shot at is nothing like the films portray. Fear kicks in; adrenaline pumps through your body. I rammed the car into gear, and raced away.

CHAPTER 3

NEW OPPORTUNITIES

Heroin is a very sneaky drug. It slowly destroys your humanity, until eventually you find yourself doing things you thought you'd never do; things that would make anyone despise themselves.

I started by smoking it just to help the comedown from ecstasy and amphetamine. But then I began to use the drug midweek. Instead of going out at the weekend, my friends and I would score some heroin and just pass out all night.

There is a weird stepping-stone process with drugs. They seem to seduce you little by little. It's like the Child Catcher from the film *Chitty Chitty Bang Bang*, luring in the kids one lollypop at a time; before they know it, they're in a cage with no hope of escape. With drugs, you start smoking weed when you're drunk and out with your mates; the buzz gets to be a little old after a while, and you want another experience. You take another step down to LSD, all the while saying, "I'll never be like one of them smackheads! I'm just doing a bit of weed, the odd tab." Then you want to experiment a bit more, just to try an E to see what it's like. By this time, you're up for anything, saying things like, "It's my body. I can do what I want with it. It's not hurting anyone." It's only now, looking back, that I see how many people it *did* hurt.

I experimented a little more, mixing amphetamine and LSD when I was out clubbing. It's a lethal combination, but I wasn't bothered because it was all about the experience. "Live hard and die young," I thought. It sounds so stupid now, but it really was how I felt. I couldn't see past the moment; I was completely consumed, moving from experience to experience.

When it comes to drug use, there are always social pecking orders and stereotypes. Heroin is seen as being at the bottom of the list. When I started using, I smoked it because that's not seen as being as bad as injecting or "digging" the drug. When I was smoking it, I remember saying, "I'll never dig it", meaning, "I will never inject." But most users – including me – do end up in that place where they are injecting, not really understanding how they got there.

I reasoned it all out to myself. Injecting was purely a practical solution at first. If I was smoking a gram of heroin a day, then by injecting it I would only need about half as much to get the same effect. This was great, as I was spending a lot of money on heroin at this point. I still remember the first "dig" I had. I was in a mate's flat; there were three of us. We "cooked up" and got our works ready ("cooking up" means that you put the heroin in a metal spoon, add a little water and some citric acid or vinegar then hold a lighter under the spoon. You draw the mix up into the syringe through a filter). I didn't even need a tourniquet as my veins were all still pronounced. As soon as I hit a vein, I drew back the plunger a little to make sure it was in. A little bit of blood fired into the barrel and I knew I was OK. I sank the plunger down slowly and a wave of tranquillity just washed over me instantly. That was it; I wasn't just addicted to heroin, but to injecting as well. Each time I injected I would be chasing a bigger, better, more powerful hit than the last time.

This new addiction would land me in hospital a few times. When you are constantly taking chances with injecting, overdose becomes inevitable. I took too many chances on too many occasions, and I can only put it down to a miracle that I am here writing this story today.

How does heroin addiction work? Something like this. When you start, you never think that it will take such a powerful hold over your life. You always believe that you will be in control, but in a very short period of time you realize that you were wrong. By that point it is too late. The human body is an amazing design; all of your muscles and nervous system are controlled by electrical impulses that you don't feel because of your body's natural painkillers. You have a ball of acid in your stomach powerful enough to eat through pretty much anything you put in there. Your skeletal system and joints are under huge amounts of pressure as you move around, but you don't feel it because of those natural painkillers. When you are using heroin, your body knows that there is an overload of painkillers in your system so it says to itself, "I may as well shut down production, because he (or she) doesn't need it." The problem then is that when the heroin wears off there are no painkillers in your system. You are now physically dependent on the drug; you need it just to function. Just to get out of bed is going to cost you £20.

This is where I found myself. I was a heroin addict. The young man full of potential was dead. All I cared about was my next fix. I was now selling heroin to feed my habit, scoring large quantities at cheaper prices to give me a larger profit, most of which would end up being injected into whichever vein was available.

The longer you inject, the more difficult it becomes, as your veins sink away. I began injecting in the arms, but as your veins disappear you start taking crazy risks, such as injecting in your neck.

After a while, a dealer further up the pecking order approached me. He would bring in very large quantities of heroin, and wanted me to go into business with him. I took up his offer. It was another of my monumental mistakes, but I did it to increase my status more than anything else. Being linked with this guy meant I had more power when I needed it – and in the world of drugs, having some backup is very important.

Living in this world means you have to do some shameful things

– for example, beating people up because they owe you £100, not because of the money, but because of the warped principle that you can't let people get away with it. I saw a guy get tied up and the bottom of his feet ripped apart with a strimmer over £300, just because he was seen to have taken liberties and been disrespectful.

I was going deeper into a world that is very hard to walk away from. It wasn't just the drug use, it was the people I was mixing with. The world of drugs really is just that – another world. Most people would have no idea how to access this world, but it all begins when you take one little step. For me (and a lot of young people) it began with cannabis. You start off by knowing someone who can score for you, and then you get to know the dealer and can score for yourself. You then start to score larger amounts so you can sell some to your mates to fund your own use. At this point, the danger is to get a larger amount to sell and make a profit. It only takes one thing to go wrong and you're in debt to a dealer. I would allow people to get in debt to me, and make them work it off. If they didn't, then they would pay – one way or another.

By now, I had witnessed and taken part in all kinds of violence for all sorts of reasons. When I look back at those times, I managed to justify every single one as it was happening. So when I began to get more heavily involved with these people I knew exactly who they were and what they were capable of. But even with all that knowledge, I had no idea what was coming next.

After agreeing to get involved with them, we set up a meet. The arrangement was for someone to come and pick me up. I thought it would just be me and the guy I was dealing with, so when the car pulled up and I saw there were two of them, I felt a little apprehensive.

The car door opened for me, and I climbed in, glancing from the dealer to the "meathead" in the passenger seat. "Where are we going?"

"We've got one more to pick up," said the dealer. "And then we'll be having a chat – to lay down some ground rules."

By now I was seriously nervous, but I wasn't going to let them know it. I sat back, and tried to look unfazed as we drove to one of the local estates.

"Right," said the dealer, as we pulled up outside a house. "Come on. You can help us pick this fella up." He turned in his seat and eyed me. "He owes us some money. We're going to make sure he pays."

"OK," I replied, as coolly as I could.

The three of us got out of the car, and walked up the path. The dealer knocked on the door.

As soon as the guy opened up, the dealer and Meathead grabbed him.

"Come on," said the dealer, grimly. "We're going for a ride."

We got in the car and sped off with a squeal of tyres. We started heading out of town and it was then that I realized where we were going.

"Oh no," I muttered under my breath.

We pulled into an old quarry. Everyone got out. The guy we'd grabbed was almost in tears, pleading with us and offering all kinds of explanations as to why he didn't have the money and how he was going to get it. But the dealer and Meathead weren't interested. They started giving the guy a good kicking. I joined in, laying into the guy with my feet, kicking his ribs and kidneys and stamping on him.

Eventually, the kicking stopped and I thought it was all over. But then the dealer went to the car. When he came back, I saw he had a huge lump hammer in his hand.

"Hold him down."

Meathead and I followed our orders. The guy was already on the ground, but we held him tight. What was going to happen? I was fully expecting the dealer to smash the guy's knees, but he stood over his head. Then he very deftly pulled the hammer up and swung it. It hit the ground no more than an inch from the side of the guy's head.

The dealer laughed. "If you cross me again," he told the terrified guy, "my aim won't be as bad."

They picked the guy up and bundled him in the car. He was a mess. I was sitting beside him in the back, and he couldn't stop talking: "I'm sorry, I'm sorry. It won't happen again. I'm sorry. I mean it. It really won't happen again."

We dropped him back on the estate and he was given a deadline to get the money together. Then we drove off.

It was then that the dealer glanced at me in the rear-view mirror.

"Darrell, if you ever try to screw me I'll give you the same and more, understand?"

I wasn't going to argue with him, and made some sort of pledge that I would never do it. Actually, I later *did* cross him, without his knowing it, and on more than one occasion. But then, I never was very good at doing as I was told.

CHAPTER 4

ARRESTED!

S o, I had a new status and a steady stream of drugs coming through. The problem was, I started using more.

There was another downside to my new status. The police had begun taking a very keen interest in me. I later discovered that they had had me under surveillance for a long time – camping out in a flat opposite mine, watching my movements. I never resented or hated the police. I always thought it was their job to catch me, and my job not to be caught. From time to time, they would arrest me just to try to scare me a little. They would tell me that they knew what I was up to, and that they had evidence to prove it. I knew they hadn't, and they would release me without charge. It was an ongoing game of cat and mouse.

Then, the police changed their approach. They arrested me for questioning about a lorry that had been stolen with a load of training shoes in the back, but while I was at the station, a CID officer approached me with an offer. The people I was now involved with were very much wanted by the police, and the cops wanted me to become an informant for them. This would mean money for me. It was tempting, but I shook my head. Why? Well, I knew that if I was discovered, it would mean my life.

The police didn't give up that easily, though. When I was arrested I'd had £500 in cash on me. This wasn't a problem until the police searched my clothing and found a very small amount of cannabis in my jeans' pocket. This was enough for them to hold my money.

"Of course, if you're willing to consider our offer," the CID officer told me, "you can have your money back."

Five hundred pounds! I couldn't let *that* go, could I?

"OK. I'll do it."

"Good lad. Here's my mobile number. You can go."

I never did get charged with any offences to do with drugs, apart from one caution. But in the end it would be my own greed that would bring me down.

In a very short period of time, things went from bad to worse. My drug addiction was spiralling out of control and my crimes were becoming more frequent. Every day I seemed to be losing more and more of myself. The more heroin took a hold of me, the more I seemed to die inside. I no longer cared about the victims of my crimes. All I cared about was having the money to feed my ever-increasing habit.

By this point I was consuming 80 mg of methadone as well as around £70 to £120-worth of heroin each day. I did try to stop on many occasions. My addiction to methadone was a result of one of my attempts to stop using. All I really wanted to do was to push the "rewind" button on my life, but by this time it was too late. I had travelled too far down the wrong road, and I felt as if there would be no return. In fact, I felt that all I had to look forward to was a sticky end.

I continued to take really stupid risks, increasing the amount of heroin I would inject just to get a bigger hit or a higher high. On a couple of occasions I overdosed, and the people I was with managed to bring me round. I was about sixteen or seventeen years old at the time. I had already lost friends and acquaintances to drugs, but I will never forget watching someone die through an overdose.

We had just got a new batch of heroin in. This stuff was different; the heroin we usually used was dark, but this was much lighter in colour and much stronger. We called it "China White". I got together with two of the main lads who were selling with me and we decided that we were going to have a "dig" before we started bagging the heroin up to drop round to the people selling for us. We had so much, everyone probably cooked up a little more than they normally would have done. And that's when things started to go wrong.

After "digging", we all passed out for a bit. But when I started to come round, I noticed that one of the lads didn't look too good. Joey wasn't someone we really knew that well; we were just using his flat because I didn't want gear in mine.

I'd seen people overdose before, so I knew what had happened. Joey's eyelids and lips had turned blue and he was deathly pale. We started trying to bring him round, but nothing was working. Eventually someone called 999, and we took Joey out of the flat and down the steps to the street.

When you're a user and this sort of thing happens, you get a feeling of complete helplessness mixed with fear and anxiety – but deep down, all you really care about is yourself and the possible trouble this could get you in. So as soon as we heard the ambulance's siren, we ran for it, thinking Joey would be OK. But he wasn't. Joey died.

By now, I had reached the point where I really did not care whether I lived or died, either. I was in self-destruct mode. Any feelings of guilt were long gone, buried beneath the addiction which was controlling me. So when I was asked to take part in an armed robbery on a wages depot, I didn't think twice. Actually, the only thought that went through my mind was, "Great! Some easy money. I wonder how much we'll get?" They wanted me to be the driver – I'd stolen plenty of cars in my time, and was a pretty good driver – and I readily agreed.

The robbery was nothing like you see in the movies. It was over in a flash, and I thought we'd got away with it. I'm not sure whether it was down to arrogance or the fact that I did not care whether I was caught or not, but that night I slept like a baby with a head full of drugs suppressing any feelings of remorse or guilt that might have been trying to creep in.

Little did I know that the next day would be the start of my life truly changing – and that change would begin with my arrest.

I was in my flat carrying on with my day as I normally would, when one of the people who sold for me knocked loudly at the door.

"Darrell!" He was out of breath. "Police – they're all over the top of the road. Dogs, the lot."

"OK." I knew straight away that they were coming for me and started to plan my escape – but that wasn't going to happen. They had armed response units, uniformed coppers and CID, but that wasn't the problem. I'd have taken my chances with them. No, the one reason for not trying to leg it was the police dogs. I already knew from a previous encounter that you didn't get away from them.

I had to come up with something else, and fast. One of my mates, Paul, had a flat just two blocks down from mine and I reckoned that I could make it there without being spotted. I grabbed the heroin I had in the flat. It was only a couple of grams because I never kept much on me just in case of a bust. (I always used to stash my gear in different places; there was an abandoned old school that was always pretty safe. Failing that, I would pay someone to hold it.) I wrapped up my gear and injecting equipment, and set off down the back stairs. All was going well till I got to Paul's. He wasn't there! I ran a hand over my face. What should I do? I couldn't go back because the police would be at my place by now. So I kicked Paul's door in, busting the lock, and darted inside. I shut the door behind me as best I could, and went to the window. I saw the police heading for my flat, and heard them break my door down. Then they started going from door to door. So I drew the curtains and cooked up some heroin.

"If I'm going to the cells, I might as well go smashed!" I thought to myself.

I injected some of the heroin, then wrapped up the rest and sealed it inside a condom. I covered that in electrical tape – and swallowed it. Then I sat down and passed out for a while.

I woke up to hear banging on the door. The police! Because I had busted the lock, the door swung open as they knocked on it. A couple of uniformed officers and a guy in plain clothes from CID came in, announcing who they were. They weren't cops I knew, and they didn't know me. So I decided to play it cool – it was time to do some acting.

I jumped up from the sofa, looking all surprised, rubbing my eyes as if I had been asleep.

"What're you doing in my flat? What's this all about?"

"Door was open, sir. Looks like your lock's broken."

"Oh yeah, yeah. Lost my keys and had to kick the door in! I'm waiting for the council to fix it. What's going on?"

"We're looking for Darrell Tunningley."

"Who? Oh, Darrell! Oh, yeah, I know Darrell. He lives up the road. I'm Paul Robson. This is my flat."

For a minute it looked like it might work. But then another officer from CID walked in. Unfortunately, he *did* know me.

"Hello, Darrell," he said.

At that point, everything went crazy.

"Move away from the knife!" they started yelling. "Move away from the knife! *Now!*"

"Eh? What knife?" Then I saw that the table beside the sofa had a kitchen knife on it.

I obviously didn't move fast enough, because the armed response guys raced in. They were all shouting as they grabbed me and pushed me face down on the carpet. Then they clamped on handcuffs, hauled me to my feet and started to march me out, explaining my rights and the charges as we walked. The cuffs were being twisted and digging into my wrists, so I started to struggle. I flung my head back – and headbutted one of the police officers. Next thing I knew, I was on the floor again, face down, and they were yelling at me to stop struggling. I eventually ended up in the back of the police van, on my way to the station. I was just seventeen and a half.

CHAPTER 5

GUILTY

I had a fair idea of what was going to happen when we arrived at Pontefract Police Station, as it wasn't my first visit. I started to think about what I was going to say – and not say. The usual drill was to keep your mouth shut until you had seen a solicitor. This usually worked, and you could count on being out and about again in a short period of time. Most people panic, thinking that they have to prove their innocence. But when you've been arrested a few times, you soon figure out that this is not the case. You don't have to prove that you are innocent. They have to prove that you are guilty.

My plan seemed to be working. I was just saying, "No comment. No comment." But what I didn't know was that the police had an ace up their sleeve. They had a witness to the robbery, and not just any old witness, but one of the lads who had been on the job and turned informant. He had been picked up before me. After detoxing in the cells for a while, he had decided to make sure he was going to be OK, and turned the rest of us in. Actually, in the end, this became irrelevant because as the police built their case against me other witnesses came forward and I was picked out from a line-up, so I was well and truly stuffed.

I had to change my plan of saying nothing and start thinking about damage control. I had to come out of this as best I could. I was being interviewed on a regular basis, and it soon became apparent that the police were more interested in my dealings with other people than they were in sending me away for what I had done. They were using all kinds of tactics to get me to give them info on the people I was involved with, but that wasn't going to happen. I knew that no matter how much they guaranteed my protection, it would never be enough. If I turned on the people I'd been working with, they would get to whoever they could in order to get at me, and there was no way the police could look after my whole family.

After a few days of appearing in front of the magistrate and being remanded back into police custody for questioning, the cops got the message that I wasn't going to cooperate. The next time I went before the magistrate, my solicitor made a request for bail. It was turned down, and I was remanded to Doncaster Prison.

By this time I was in a really bad way. I was detoxing from heroin and methadone with nothing to help ease the symptoms. I hadn't slept and I was in all kinds of pain. One of the side-effects of heroin addiction is constipation so I hadn't passed the heroin I had swallowed. I was hoping that it was wrapped up well enough to survive until I could get processed and onto the wing. I saw the doctor in the reception of the prison and explained my condition. He gave me a laxative, so I couldn't wait to get on the wing. It was about 9 p.m. when I was put in a double cell with a guy I didn't know. Without going into too much detail, the laxative did its job and I retrieved the parcel.

The guy I was banged up with proved useful. He had some matches and silver foil – wrapping from a KitKat bar. This was all I needed. As I unwrapped the parcel, I was thrilled that the heroin had survived. The relief was almost instant. I sat and smoked until I felt what I believed to be normal again, sorting out my new cell-mate with a few lines for supplying the foil and matches.

When I'd come in through reception, I'd had a choice of having a phone card or half an ounce of tobacco. I chose the phone card as I knew I would get smokes on the wing, and I needed to make a call as soon as I could. I had kept my mouth shut to the police and made a "not guilty" plea at the magistrates' court. I knew this meant I would get extra privileges while on remand – if you plead guilty, then you are immediately classed as a con. One of the extra perks I could expect was more association time out of my cell and a chance to use the phone.

After breakfast and morning roll call, we were let out for association. I made a very short phone call to the main guy I had been dealing with. The calls were monitored so I simply said, "It's all good. There's nothing to worry about from my end." He replied, "Nice one." That was it. Keeping my mouth shut meant I was in no danger and could just get on with my time. But I didn't know yet how much time that would be. I knew that the drugs I had would not last long, and there was no way of getting enough brought in to sustain my level of habit. I was going to have to go through detox. I had done it before, so I knew how bad it was, and I wasn't looking forward to it at all.

I went to see the doctor again. At that time, the prison didn't offer a medicated detox. All they had were tablets that I hadn't come across before; the lads called them "Black Stars". They were supposed to speed up the whole process and so get it over with faster. "Oh well," I thought, "the faster the better." I decided to sell a little of the heroin and get myself some tobacco, phone cards, shower gel, and plenty of biscuits and juice – all forms of currency inside. I'd have enough of the drug left for one last night, and that would be it.

A detox from heroin isn't something that's easy to describe. Depending on how much heroin you have been using, it can range from fairly manageable – like a bad dose of flu – to pretty unbearable. Unfortunately, I was looking at the second option. The worst thing about detoxing isn't the vomiting, the agonizing stomach cramps, or the pain in your legs that feels as if someone is breaking them over and over again. No; the worst thing is that you can't sleep because of it all. Through the day there are distractions, people to talk to, you can try to move around to help the muscle pains. But at night it's just you and the pain for twelve hours.

I wasn't doing well at all. By day three I was a wreck, so I saw the doctor. "You'll be OK," he told me, briefly. "A detox won't kill you." But that night it became too much to bear.

I remember lying in my bunk, trying to sleep and getting up to go to the toilet. I suddenly felt an excruciating pain in my left side, then nothing. I woke up in the hospital wing of the prison with my head pounding, still feeling as bad as ever. One of the prison officers said I had collapsed and whacked my head on the sink. My cell-mate had hit the alarm button and they found me unconscious on the floor.

It turned out that the doctor hadn't been right in his thirty-second prognosis. They told me that my body had simply gone on strike because it couldn't cope with the amount of toxins it was trying to process. I remember saying, "Oh well, at least I got some sleep!"

I spent the next couple of weeks on the hospital wing. By then I was beginning to feel something close to normal. My appetite had come back with a vengeance; I was eating everything I could get my hands on, and putting on weight quickly. This was not a bad thing as I went into prison weighing about nine and a half stone. As I'm 6ft 2in tall, I looked terrible.

As I started to settle back into the normal grind of prison life, I got a job as a cleaner on the wing, which kept me out of the cell and busy. Prison life is never dull, and Doncaster at the time had a poor record when it came to violence, self-harm and suicide. Every week someone would slash their wrists or try to hang themselves; sometimes they succeeded. There was one occasion when a lad who was being badly bullied went to his window, stuck his arms out and slashed them. Everyone on his landing put their shaving mirrors out of their windows to watch this guy try to kill himself, cheering him on, encouraging him to do it. Fortunately he didn't succeed, but he really made a mess of himself.

I'm ashamed to say that I joined in with the cheering. When you lose your humanity, then you know you're in a bad place. My own encounters with violence inside had calmed down after I had made it clear that I would do whatever it took to win a fight. In prison, everything is about saving face and being respected, and that means hurting people to get what you need.

The need to prove myself soon came up. Not long after coming back on the wing after my stay in hospital, a couple of lads came up to me in the association area.

"We know you're getting visits and you better sort us out," they said. They had heard I was bringing drugs in and wanted me to give some to them. I was standing near the pool table with the bigger of the two lads closest to me. Without saying a word I grabbed a pool ball in my hand and flew at the big guy, smashing him repeatedly over the head. The smaller of the two ran off.

"Who do you think you're talking to?" I yelled, as I continued hitting the guy on the floor.

The screws soon came and dragged me away. It cost me a week in "the block" but I didn't have any more challenges when I got back on the wing. ("The block" was a separate unit away from the main prison population.)

I was still on remand, and was facing a trial if I didn't change my plea. After speaking with my barrister, I realized that my best option was to plead guilty. So that's what I did. I was told what was going to happen and to expect up to ten years.

On the day I was taken to Leeds Crown Court I was still behaving like an idiot, mostly to hide the fact that I was shaking inside. In the holding cell on my own, waiting for what was coming, I convinced myself that I would take it like a man. I was taken up to the dock and told to stand as the judge came in. He was an angry-looking guy. In fact, he had an expression on his face that said "I would rather be somewhere else", which did not fill me with confidence.

I had changed my plea to guilty so there was no jury, just people in the viewing area, my barrister, and the prosecution. My barrister was court-appointed. She was a youngish woman, and I thought it seemed as if she hadn't been doing the job too long. The barrister for the prosecution, on the other hand, looked as if he had been doing this for a very long time and had not a second to waste. He put the case before the judge and made me look like a psychotic piece of scum who should never see the light of day again – not that he used those exact words, of course, but you get the picture.

Then my barrister got up, rustling her papers, and I thought, "Now she'll turn it around. She'll tell them that I'm not all that bad; just a misled youth who should have a second chance." That's what I thought would happen – but it didn't. She said that as I had pleaded guilty she didn't have much more to add! I couldn't believe what I was hearing. Even the judge told her off, saying that it was her job to defend and present a case regardless of the plea. She apologized to the judge and said something about taking my age into account as I was just eighteen and I could have a bright future.

I sat back, thinking, "You're stuffed, mate!" Then I was asked if I would like to say anything before the judge considered my sentence. So I stood up and tried to put on the most apologetic face I could. I must have looked like Oliver standing there, saying, "Please, sir!" In my pleading voice I basically said, "I'm a good boy, honest, and I'll never do it again!" What a lie. I was sorry I'd been caught and that was about it, but obviously I wasn't about to tell the judge that.

After my Oscar-winning performance I was taken back to the holding cells while the judge considered my fate. I'm not sure how long I was down there, but it seemed like hours. When I finally heard the key turn in the lock I got up, telling myself that I was ready for what was coming. I was taken back up to court three, and stood in the dock. I was told to remain standing as the judge said his part.

It started really well, with the judge being positive. He was agreeing with my barrister that I was a young man with a bright future, if I could turn away from drugs and crime. I couldn't believe my ears and started to think that I might get a lenient sentence, but then the tone of his voice changed and he said that the severity of my crimes demanded a custodial sentence. My legs started to feel like jelly, I was sweating like crazy, and for a moment I lost track of what he was saying. Then he said that he had intended to give me a seven-year sentence, but he was going to give me a second chance. I received a total of five and a half years for my crimes.

It was a lot less than I was expecting, but still, the thought of years locked away hit me hard.

After sentencing I went back down to the holding cells and I was told I would be able to speak to my family. They brought me to a cubicle with a glass screen and told me to wait. Everything was still sinking in and I was using all my strength just to hold it together. I couldn't let anyone see what was going on inside, that I felt as if I was ready to snap.

My family came in and stood on the other side of the glass. I could see that they were upset. My mum and dad's eyes were red. I knew right then that I had to show them that I was OK.

"Be strong," my dad was saying, "and keep your chin up."

"I'll be fine," I replied, as coolly as I could. "The time'll fly by. I've learned my lesson. I'll be out before you know it."

It was one of the hardest things I had ever had to do, but somehow I managed to stay calm, and after a while I was taken back to a holding cell.

The door locked and I sat on the bench for a few minutes just feeling numb. Then I exploded, shouting, screaming and kicking the walls and the door. Strangely, after a while the numbness came over me again; I calmed right down and sat there, not thinking, as I waited for the "sweatbox" to take me back to Doncaster.

The only thing that clearly stuck in my mind from what the judge said as he summed up was, "Your future is in your hands." He was almost right. I did have a future; there was a plan, but in truth it wasn't in my hands at all. It was in the hands of God.

CHAPTER 6

INSIDE

The first part of my life as a con was spent figuring out what I could and couldn't get away with, where the boundaries could be pushed and rules broken, trying to make the best of a bad situation. Sometimes the press seems to paint prison as a bit of a holiday camp, but my own experience was very different. When I was inside, I didn't have a TV in my cell; I didn't even have a kettle.

The prison had a three-tiered system: basic, standard and enhanced. When you first "landed", you were put on standard – you were given so many visiting orders (or VOs) and a certain amount of time out of your cell. You could have access to certain jobs and educational courses, and you could spend £15 in the canteen, if you had any money sent in. Enhanced meant that you were given longer visiting times, more association time out of your cell, and you could spend more cash, if you had it. You also had opportunities to access better work placements. The basic level was just that; you got the bare minimum. Starting on standard meant you could choose your own level of living inside; if you behaved you went up, and if you didn't, you went down.

I was still a criminal. I had that mentality. So I made a decision. If I was going to be a con, then I would be the best con I could be. Every swindle, every deal I could be involved in or make money from, then I would be right there. This meant that I got into a lot of trouble and floated between basic and standard levels for quite a while. It wasn't all about fighting and violence; I did silly things as well.

On one occasion, I rigged up my next-door neighbour, Billy, to my power supply as he was on basic regime at the time and had no batteries for his radio. We did it by getting one of the lads who was doing a course over in the education block to nick a twelve-volt adaptor, and another lad to nick some wire from the workshops. I then rigged a power supply through a small gap in the heating pipe that ran between our cells. All was going well until I went to the gym and left the power on for Billy. The screws (prison warders) decided to spin my pad (search my cell) for contraband while I was away; actually, they were only supposed to do this while the inmate was present. When I came back my cell was upside down, and the power supply had gone.

I was given a "nicking notice" to appear in front of the governor in the morning. The charge had been written up by a female officer. She said she had noticed a wire through the window of my cell door and had searched under my bed to discover the rigged power supply. I was furious because they had "spun my pad" without me being there. I also knew they were lying about how they had spotted the wire to cover the fact that they had broken the rules.

When I appeared in front of the governor, he read out the charges. Then he raised his eyes and asked me if I had anything to say. Anything to say? You bet I did!

"Our beds are about twelve inches from the floor," I began, looking at the well-built female accusing officer. I then pointed out that there was no way a woman of her size could possibly have fitted under the bed to discover any wiring. I wasn't polite when I said all of this, and the female officer left the room, crying. Not a good move, as the governor was just going to dock me a week's wages. Now he decided to dock me for two weeks, and give me two weeks in the block as well. My mouth and anger had got me in trouble again.

The block was not a nice place. Different prisons had different systems, but it generally meant you were on twenty-four hour lockdown, sometimes with an hour in a very small exercise yard every other day. In one prison I was in, they took the mattress off the bed in the morning and gave it back in the evening; all you had was a little metal toilet, a sink, a chair, and a book if you were lucky. In every prison I was in, I had a visit to the block. I had some short stays, and some longer ones. But it meant that I was developing a reputation with the inmates and prison officers.

On the wing, things were pretty comfortable for me. Lending tobacco for double the amount back meant I had plenty of currency. People would get into debt with me and would pay me back in various ways – phone cards, canteen orders, or by taking visits from people who'd bring in drugs.

One guy I'd known for years – I went to school with him – had taken a visit. Everyone knew his visitor was bringing drugs in, and everybody also knew the rule: If you brought drugs onto the wing, you had to sort Darrell and a few of the other lads out first. But he told the screws he was sick and didn't come out of his cell for a few days, except at meal times. I knew I had to do something about the situation, but I had to wait until I had a chance. That chance came about a week later. We were walking back from the gym and he was behind me. In a split second, I spun around and hit him, breaking his jaw. He fell to the ground, and we all just carried on walking as if nothing had happened. I did feel a little guilty, as I hadn't intended to break his jaw, and he ended up on a liquid diet for about six weeks as a result of it; but that's just what you had to do inside if you were going to have any kind of respect from the other lads.

As it became harder to bring drugs in through visits, we came up with more creative ideas. While in HMP Doncaster we noticed that the lads on yard-cleaning duty were not searched as they came back on the wing. We found a way to take advantage of this – by using dead birds. More often than not there would be a couple of dead pigeons on the yard. So we arranged to have dead pigeons stuffed with drugs catapulted over the wall into the exercise yard. The yard cleaners would go out to do their job, conceal the drugs, and bring them back onto the wing.

Life went on like this for a while, and I was moved around the country a fair bit. I went from Doncaster to Leeds, which wasn't too bad as it was still in Yorkshire and I could still get visits. Then I was moved to Glen Parva in Leicester, a couple of hundred miles from anyone I knew, and too far away to get regular visits. This prison was probably the worst one of them all. It had an old-style three-tier landing, and if you weren't working or in education (and there were no places in either), a routine of twenty-three and twenty-four hour lockdown, which meant you got an hour out of your cell every other day. The food was terrible, too. Once I got mashed potato scooped onto my metal food tray, and I could still see the tray through the mash! Every night they came round with a tea urn and took our dirty food trays away, and that was it till the following morning.

Because we were in our cells so much, my cell-mate and I would come up with some crazy ways to entertain ourselves. We once fashioned boxing gloves out of towels and took it in turns hitting each other on the head. First one to give up, lost! The cells had holes round the heating pipes that ran through the walls and we could just about see through to the cells on either side of us. We would use these to distribute drugs and other contraband. We were on the twos (or second landing), so people would make a line from strips of bedding, lower it down to us from their window, and then it would be passed along to whoever wanted it. The night clocky (prison officer on night duty) would listen out for contraband being passed about. One of them used to take his shoes off, and try to sneak around in his socks. We used to have fun feeding him misinformation.

One night, we rigged up a water channel from shiny magazine covers and ran it from our tap to the hole which led into the next cell. We waited until lights out, and then slowly started the water running. After a while it started flowing under the cell door. The night clocky came round and hit the alarm, thinking they had flooded the cell. We quickly disposed of any evidence and giggled as our "next-door neighbours" were dragged away protesting their innocence.

I've said this prison was the worst one of all; it really was nasty. When they turned the lights off at night, we had to move our shoes and anything else off the floor because the cockroaches would all scurry out. While I was there, the prison was inspected. It was supposed to be a week-long inspection, but the inspectors left after two days telling them to sort the place out or they would shut it down.

As soon as I had arrived at the prison, I had started putting in transfer requests to be moved closer to home. It took a few months, but eventually my transfer came through. My new "home" would be Wolds Prison, near Hull. I hadn't a clue what it would be like, as I didn't know anyone who had been in that prison. But surely, I thought, it had to be better than Glen Parva!

CHAPTER 7

RESPECT

I t took almost three hours in a sweatbox to reach HMP Wolds. This was a privately run prison, owned by Group 4 Prison Services, a private company that runs prisons and court security instead of the government. I knew that this usually meant a better deal for the prisoner, but I wasn't expecting anything good; in truth, I didn't really know *what* to expect.

Still, I knew it was different as soon as we hit the prison reception area. They put us in a holding room and asked if we wanted a cup of tea! When they arrived back with a tea trolley loaded with packets of biscuits, I was happy.

We went through the usual routine of filling in forms, checking belongings, a medical examination and a search, then off we went to our cells. As soon as we started walking through the prison I could see it was very different from anything I'd experienced before, and when we arrived on the wing and I spotted a snooker table and two pool tables as well as a TV room, I couldn't believe my luck. Sure, it was still a Category A prison, but compared to where I had come from it might as well have been a Hilton Hotel.

I was taken up to the first floor, and we walked down to the corner cell. When the prison officer told me, "You're in a single cell", I couldn't believe my ears. I had never had a single cell before. I was used to being crammed into cells designed for one, but usually holding two or three. A cell to myself – great! It even had a kettle. The prison officer came back with what we called a "brew pack", filled with tea bags, sugar and powdered milk, so I sat and had a brew in private.

My cell looked out over a walkway with just the fences and wall behind it. I was standing at the window when suddenly I noticed that it was strangely quiet. Apart from a couple of radios, there was no noise at all. I had been used to spending my evenings listening to people arguing, insulting each other's mums, or just bullying someone in the next cell. But there was nothing. I sorted out all my things and went to bed.

The next day, the prison routine began. I was woken up, and went down for breakfast; we had our own plastic cutlery, so I took mine down to the canteen and joined the queue. In this prison, Saturday was cooked breakfast day – porridge, bacon, sausage, egg, beans and toast – so I sat down at the seat allocated to my cell, and tucked into the best breakfast I had eaten in a long time.

The table slowly filled up, and then came the usual "sussing each other out" – "What you in for?", "How long you got?" – that kind of thing. In prison, once you've figured out that the guy you're talking to isn't inside for anything dodgy (such as child molesting), you then move on to working out if you know anybody they know. As long as you know enough people, or they have heard of you, then you're OK – and that was the case for me on this occasion. One of the lads had been inside with one of my co-accused, so already knew all about me. This was good news, as I wouldn't have to go through the process of proving how hard I was.

I soon discovered that most of the people in Wolds were on longer-term sentences, usually five years and more. That was why there was a relaxed kind of feel to the place; most of the guys had been in prison for a while and just wanted to get their heads down, do their time and get out.

I had to go on an induction course, and when I went through the assessment to see what level I was at, it turned out I was pretty smart! I applied for a place in the workshops as I had been told it was an easy option and you got £17.50 per week. In prison that was a good wage. I couldn't believe it when, by the Monday, I had a place in the welding shop. Things were good and that was how it stayed for a while – nice and quiet.

Now that I had figured out who were the right people to have onside, who not to associate with, and who would be beneficial to me, I could sort out getting hold of some drugs. I would either ask someone to visit, or use somebody who was already set up with a visit. All I needed to do was to get one of my mates on the outside to meet up with the person doing the smuggling, and give them the package to bring in. Once the drugs were inside the prison, I would give some to the person organizing the smuggler, and everyone would be happy. One phone call, a couple of days waiting for the visit, and that was it – enough drugs for myself, and some to sell on to make a bit of money.

Life was comfortable. I had settled down so I wasn't getting in as much trouble as I had before, and I had everything I could need for a life in prison. I had no idea that something was about to happen that would change everything.

It was a day like any other; same routine – screws banging on doors to wake us up, get washed, shaved and dressed, get opened up for breakfast, then off to the workshop. I was working away at my bench, making a hanging basket and chatting away to my mates when one of the other lads in the shop came up to me. He wasn't someone I associated with; he was what we called a "muppet" – someone with no status or influence at all.

"What do you want?" I turned to him with just enough aggression in my voice to let him know that I wasn't impressed by his presence.

He looked nervous. "Um – do you wanna go on an Alpha course?" he asked, quickly.

"Eh?" I had no clue what he was talking about. They were always trying to sign us up for education courses; maybe that was what he was talking about. "What's an Alpha course?"

What he said next made me laugh. He started to explain that the Alpha course was about Christianity and it was in the chapel, but that's as far as he got. As soon as I heard the word "Christianity" I wasn't interested.

"Get out of my face before I give you a slap," I told him, and I'm sure he knew he'd get more than just a slap. He didn't say another word and shot off so fast that he reminded me of the cartoon mouse, Speedy Gonzales. I made a joke of it with the other lads, making fun of the "God squad" and Bible bashers. There were always people who "found God" in prison, and I generally thought they were nut jobs.

The day ended and I thought no more about it. The next day came, the same routine started and, to my amazement, this lad was going around the workshop asking people to go on the Alpha course.

He came over to me again. I'd told him yesterday, in front of everyone, that I would slap him. Coming to me again meant he was going to get just that. I was just about to give him a smack, when he blurted out something that stopped me: "You get out of bang-up on Wednesday afternoon and there's free coffee and biscuits!"

Well, that got my attention. "Oh really?" I said. This was good news! Usually on Wednesday afternoons everyone was stuck in their cells because of staff training; we would get banged up after lunch and have to stay there until tea time. (And that was tough if you were on a basic regime, because it meant no evening association time; you were locked up until the next morning.)

In prison there is only one thing better than a freebie, and that's getting out of bang-up. All I had to do was roll along to this course run by the Bible bashers, eat biscuits and drink coffee. Great! I rounded up a few more people from the workshop to come with me. I guess that's what I'd call evangelism, now; but back then, I just wanted to get a few more people in on this so they could dodge bang-up and I wouldn't be on my own!

Wednesday arrived. We went to the workshop in the morning, then came back on the wing. We were locked up for roll call, and then let out for lunch. When lunch was over, the screws started to lock everyone away, when the chaplain came on the wing.

The PO (principal officer) shouted, "Everyone going on the Alpha course, wait by the gate!"

Grinning, I headed for the gate. "Enjoy your bang-up, lads!"

One of the wing officers walked us over to the chapel, along with the chaplain. I hadn't been in the chapel before, but it was kind of what I had expected – rows of chairs with an altar and a big cross at the front. What I *hadn't* expected were the people who had come in to run the course – two elderly nuns! If I'd had to paint a picture of a "Christian" at this point in my life, it would have been cardigans, sandals and socks – you get the idea. But nuns … well, what really amazed me was, I had never seen anybody who looked so old. Everything in me was telling me to walk away and just do the bang-up, but just then the coffee and biscuits arrived, and not just any old biscuits either, but Chocolate HobNobs! That was it. I was staying.

The women and the chaplain introduced themselves and gave us a talk about the Alpha course and what it was all about. The main gist of it was this: You could ask questions about God and life and all of that stuff and be given straight answers. I just thought, "What can these people possibly teach me about life? They've never lived through the things I have, so how can they help me?"

Just as these thoughts were running through my head, one of them rolled in a TV and video player on a stand. They showed us a pre-recorded talk by a guy named Nicky Gumbel. We all stayed quiet and listened, but in my mind I was switching off. This posh-sounding bloke on the TV was making sense, but I just kept thinking, "What does he know about life?" (These days, there are Alpha courses specially designed for every occasion – for students, youth, the workplace, the Forces, and for prisons – but back then, it was a "one size fits all".)

Then came a chance for questions and discussion. I had been getting slowly wound up by these posh do-gooders, so when my chance came I opened my mouth and let them have it. The thing that surprised me was that they didn't react. They remained totally calm as they answered every single thing I threw at them. So I decided to up my game. I become offensive, insulting, but still they came back with answers, staying cool and confident.

Our time came to an end and we had to go back to the wing. I had thrown all sorts of questions and opinions at these people who I thought knew nothing about life, and they had answered every single one of them. That night in my cell, I carried on thinking about what had happened on the course. It wasn't so much what was said, but how they had said it. They had responded to me in a way that I wasn't used to. In prison, I was used to demanding respect from others through fear and intimidation, but they had shown us all a different kind of respect. It was weird, but it felt as if they genuinely cared about each and every one of us.

CHAPTER 8

ALL NEW!

The next session came around and we followed the same routine, queuing at the gate after lunch and being escorted to the chapel. A couple of the lads from the workshop had decided it wasn't for them, but I wanted to fire off some more questions. I was determined to catch these Christians out.

We sat down and had our coffee and biscuits – custard creams this time. Then the TV came out and Nicky Gumbel started his talk. It was about Jesus.

Now, I already believed in God. I didn't need any convincing on that score. But my idea of God was the one I had been given through school assemblies and religious education. God was someone or something that had created everything we see around us; that's as far as my understanding went. But the whole Jesus issue – well, that was another story for me. I'd always thought of Him as a good guy who had done good things. And I guess I thought that people – Christians – tried to do what He did so that they could be good too. But they started to explain that Jesus wasn't just a good man, He's God in the flesh. They said that He'd come to earth for one purpose: to put all the things right that I, Darrell, had ever done wrong. This got my attention.

We looked at loads of historical evidence, and at the things Jesus did and said. In prison, you become a bit of a legal expert, and you swap deposition papers and look at each other's cases. What I could see from the evidence about Jesus was that everything pointed to one fact: Jesus was who He'd said He was! It was amazing. These people who I thought had hidden away from life and didn't know anything were showing me something I thought was not possible – that God cared about *me*.

The second part of the session was all about how and why Jesus had died. We all knew the story from school, but for me it was just that, a story, until now. I couldn't argue my point of view that Jesus was merely a good guy any more, because everything about Him, everything He did, everything He said, meant that He was either the Son of God, or an absolute nut job. And when they began showing us how Jesus had died it really hit home.

For a start, it really struck me that He didn't have to go back to Jerusalem. He knew what they were going to do to Him there, and He walked right into it on purpose. If that were me, I wouldn't have gone back; I'd have legged it. It would be like a gang having money on your head and you purposely walking around on their patch. You just don't do it! The second thing that got me was that He knew He was going to be crucified. This is the sickest way of killing people that humankind has ever dreamt up. It was so bad that eventually the Romans gave it up and went back to impaling, because it was quicker and kinder! The third thing that struck me was, why? I knew what it felt like to stand in a dock and have a sentence passed down. It hits you like a brick in the face and you feel like your legs are going to give way. Jesus had a sentenced passed down, but He was innocent; I suddenly saw and understood that He took the sentence for all the wrong things *I* have ever done and would ever do. It was like me turning up for sentencing to be told I could go free because someone else had volunteered to do the time.

All of a sudden I saw my life as a DVD. But it wasn't just the action, the things I'd done, or the edited highlights. No. On that DVD was all the stuff I'd ever said, as well. And all the stuff I'd ever *thought*. We all might say we'd be happy to run a DVD of our lives in front of our friends and family, but I saw right then that that wasn't true. Because if the DVD of our lives had all our words and thoughts on it … If you're anything like me, then you would want that DVD to be destroyed.

Jesus had never done anything wrong, never thought anything wrong, or said anything wrong. There wasn't a single fault in Him. His DVD would be a U rating, suitable for all audiences. But that day, in the chapel, I realized that Someone took the sentence Darrell deserved; it was a death sentence. And Jesus took it – for me.

It was all making sense to me. Because of what He had done on the cross, my DVD could be wiped. It was like I had a second chance, a clean slate; no matter what anyone else thought of me, He'd cared enough to take my sentence.

By this point I was gobsmacked. I had decided that my life was a mess and always would be, but now I was being told that I could have a fresh start.

The course continued, and I kept on coming week after week with more and more questions. Each one was answered in a way that made sense to me. We covered everything about the Bible, prayer and the Church, and we were always allowed to express our opinions.

By the end of the course, I seemed to have more questions than when I started, but of course I had also been given loads of really good answers. They gave each of us a Bible and some little booklets about being a Christian.

"Thanks," I said, seriously, as I took them all. "I'll be at church on Sunday, promise." Then I grinned. "As long as there are more biscuits!"

That night I sat in my cell. There was nothing on the radio worth listening to, so I started to flick through some of the booklets I had been given. One of them had something on the back called "The Sinner's Prayer". It sounded a bit scary. Still, I read through it and got what it was trying to say – that I needed to ask Jesus personally to forgive me – but it wasn't saying it in the way I spoke; it was as though someone else was speaking for me. So I put the booklets to one side and picked up the Bible.

We had looked at bits from the Bible, mainly about Jesus in the New Testament, but I had never had one or really read it. I started flicking through it, and eventually I came across something that caught my attention. It was the book of Job in the Old Testament. I started reading. It was an easy-to-read modern translation in plain English, so I got the gist of it pretty easily. The book of Job was about a guy who had everything – he was loaded – but the devil took everything he had, to try to make him turn his back on God. As I read on, I was engrossed. It didn't matter what was thrown at him, Job just would not turn his back on God. So in the end, God stopped the devil and gave Job back everything he had, and even more.

I sat back, shut my eyes, and started thinking. What made God so real to Job that no matter what was thrown at him, he just wouldn't budge? I was sure I must be missing out on something. I had heard all about Jesus and I believed it all, but there must be more. Believing in God changed Job's life, so why wasn't it changing mine?

I got the booklet out again and I mumbled "The Sinner's Prayer", but it didn't feel personal. It kind of felt fake somehow, so I put it down and said the first real prayer I had ever said in my life.

"All right, God. I believe. Jesus, I believe You took my sentence, that You died for me. I'm tired of feeling worthless, being an addict and being angry all the time. Take away all my anger, take my drug addiction, and take away all this mess that I've made. If You do that for me, then I'll do what You want me to do for the rest of my life."

That's the clean version. I swore a couple of times, but that's how I spoke, that was real to me, it was how I was feeling, it was where I was in my life – and God met me there. You see, God isn't looking for perfection. He loves us so much that He will take us exactly as we are. But He loves us too much to leave us that way.

I don't know what I was expecting, but nothing happened. The cell door didn't start to shake, there were no bright lights, no angel came down and no booming voice said, "Yes, My son, I can hear you." I just went to bed hoping that He had heard me.

The next morning I woke up before the screws had started banging the doors to wake everyone, so it was very quiet. What happened next was a series of events that I will never forget.

I would always make a smoke before going to bed so I could just roll over and have a cigarette before getting up. I was always gagging for a smoke in the morning. This morning, I rolled over to get the cig – but the sight of it made me feel sick! I don't mean a little groggy, I mean I couldn't stand to even look at it. I grabbed it and threw it out of my window. I couldn't shake the feeling, so I grabbed all my tobacco and threw that out of the window, too. Immediately, I started feeling better.

If I woke up early enough, I would have a spliff out of the window before the screws came. But as soon as that thought popped into my head, the horrible feeling came back worse than before. I took the little bit of weed I had and threw that out of the window as well. As soon as it had gone, I started to feel OK again.

I was freaking out by this point, and wondering what was wrong with me. I went over to the sink to start getting washed and shaved when a new feeling started to come over me. At first it was a nice warm feeling – I was happy but had no idea why – and the feeling kept on intensifying. I had had pretty much every drug going, but what I was feeling was more powerful than any of them. It was as if someone had unscrewed the top of my head and poured freezing cold water in. I could feel it running through me, washing everything bad away – all the anger and guilt and frustration. I looked at myself in the mirror and almost didn't recognize my own reflection. I was smiling and happy. All the anger that used to feel like a cancer eating me from the inside out had gone. I couldn't fully explain how all this was happening, but I knew God had heard my prayer. I knew He had forgiven me, I knew I had been given a second chance, that I was new inside.

When the prison officers came and opened our cells for breakfast,

I stepped out onto the landing still buzzing from this amazing feeling. One of my mates, who was standing next to me, took one look at my face and said, "What's up with you?"

I didn't know how to explain it, so I just said, really enthusiastically, "I don't know. I'm just happy!" He looked at me as though I had flipped and needed to be moved to a padded cell!

It was such a dramatic change, it is difficult to describe. The day before, I had come back onto the wing from the chapel, and found that the prison officers had already opened up our cells. I noticed a guy walking away from the direction of mine. When I got up there, I noticed my T-shirts had shifted on my shelf. I had stuffed a large bar of Cadbury's Dairy Milk behind them and it was missing! I instantly flipped out. I took two large LR20 batteries out of my radio, put them in a sock and went looking for this guy. He was out walking around the yard, so I waited until he was in the blind spot for the CCTV cameras, then I came up behind him, shouted his name and swung with my home-made cosh. I left him unconscious and bleeding and just walked back onto the wing. It turned out that he hadn't even taken the chocolate; one of my mates had hidden it under my pillow as a wind-up.

In prison you have to put in an application form for everything and anything, so I went to the PO's office for an application to see the chaplain. I wrote on the application:

I need to see you, please, because I think God has changed me!

Normally it would be a couple of days before it was processed and you got a response, but I went to the workshop and was only in there for half an hour when the chaplain turned up. He pulled me out of work and we went to the chapel, where I sat down and explained everything that had happened the night before and that morning.

At this point, the chaplain got really excited and explained to me what had happened. He showed me parts of the Bible that helped explain how God changes us from the inside out. One piece stuck with me straight away. It was from a book called 2 Corinthians in the New Testament, and chapter 5 verse 17, where it says: "This means that anyone who belongs to Christ has become a new person. The old life is gone; a new life has begun!" (NLT) It summed up exactly how I was feeling – all new!

CHAPTER 9

CHANGING

In prison you don't have much, so the things you do have you hold onto tightly. One of those things is your word. Back then, if I said I was going to do something I would follow it all the way through, regardless of what might happen, because I had given my word. Yes, your word was one of the few things that nobody could take from you. Until this point, it had always meant something negative – like if I said, "I'm going to break your jaw!" it wasn't an idle threat. I meant it. I chose my words carefully, so when I'd told God I would do what He wanted for the rest of my life, I really did mean it. Now I just had to figure out what it was He wanted.

God had forgiven me, given me an amazing gift of a new and eternal life, and He had overcome my drug addiction. He had changed me, inside. I had needed a miracle to put me right, and He had done it. He had answered my prayer and given me that miracle. This didn't mean, of course, that I had become perfect. There were (and still are) plenty of things that God needed to work through with me. I was soon to see that being a Christian doesn't mean we will never face problems, hardship or issues in our lives ever again. It means that when those things come along, we will overcome them;

we will face them with a new strength of mind, heart and spirit that we didn't have before.

To put it simply, from this point on I knew God had my back.

I was jam-packed full of excitement and enthusiasm, but I didn't know what to do with it. I tried to make people see that God had really changed me, and I was telling anyone who would listen about what God had done in me. The problem was that everyone knew me for being a certain way, so they had no idea how to react to me now.

One of the first things I did was to give away all my tobacco. Looking back it sounds like a funny thing to do, encouraging people to smoke. But it was a statement to everyone that I had changed. I was the "Baccy Baron" on the wing – I would lend it out for double back. I walked out on the landing the day after Jesus had given me a fresh start, and shouted, "Anyone that's got my baccy can have it!" Nobody could believe it, but it certainly got their attention. Another thing that changed was this: People were still taking visits and following the rule that if you brought drugs in, you sorted Darrell out with some. But now, when they came to me I was turning them away, saying, "I'm not interested. I don't do drugs any more."

Turning my back on my old ways was a big risk, because it meant that people would be more willing to push their luck and try to have a go at me to increase their own status. To start with, people were cautious around me, interested in what I had to say but not sure if the change was permanent. I knew that God had really changed me. There were things that God had needed to fix straight away – I had turned my back on drugs (and even today the thought of them brings back that same sick feeling), but my second biggest issue was my anger.

We were out in the exercise yard and, as usual, I was talking about what God had done in my life. One of the lads started mouthing off to me in front of everyone, and got right up in my face. I could feel my anger rising. It was like my blood was boiling and this black curtain was coming down over my mind. I could visualize what I wanted to do to this guy. I was running through it in my head. My hands were shaking with the adrenaline. I was really wound up, and ready to snap, when something inside me said, "You're not that person any more. You're new."

As soon as I heard that small voice, I started to calm down. I turned and started to walk away. Every step I took was making me calmer and calmer, until that same feeling I had experienced in my cell washed over me and I was all happy again! One of my mates helped at this point. As I walked away, he stepped in and said to the guy, "He might have changed, but I haven't. So do one or I'll do you!"

Usually I would let the anger take over, I would end up hurting the person more than I needed to, and then feel bad about myself. But now I knew I would never fight again. I felt good about myself. I saw it as a test. For the first time I had flipped the coin and come out on God's side, and it felt great. I suddenly remembered my dad telling me, "It takes a bigger man to walk away." I'd never got that until this moment. I had always thought that if I was left standing, then I was the bigger man. I was starting to realize what being a real man was all about – not throwing your weight around to prove you're hard, but walking away because you had nothing to prove to anyone but God.

A couple of weeks after Jesus had first turned my life around, another event happened that I did not see coming. It's easy, now, to see that God was in charge the whole time, but back then it was all out of the blue.

One morning, I woke up and started reading my Bible. (One good thing about prison is, you get loads of time to read and pray.) Then my cell door opened. I looked up, surprised. I wasn't expecting this, because it wasn't breakfast yet. The PO stood there and my initial thought was, "This can't be good." He threw me a couple of clear prison sacks and said, "Start getting your stuff together; you're going to Buckley Hall tomorrow."

"Buckley Hall?" I repeated.

Every prisoner pretty much knows about every other prison, the good ones, the bad ones, and also what category each prison is. I was

Category A so I was in a Category A prison. If you were good enough, you might get transferred to a Category B. But Buckley Hall at this time was a Category C prison run my Group 4, and it had a good reputation. I knew there was no way you went from Category A to C, just like that.

"I can't go to Buckley Hall," I protested. "It's a Cat C."

"Don't argue," replied the PO. "Just have your stuff ready."

I knew that the prison service had made mistakes in the past. People had packed up their stuff, moved out, the prison had realized their mistake, and by then, the prisoner had lost his cell. And I liked my single cell.

I got all my things together and the next morning after breakfast I was taken down to the reception area. I was still expecting them to say, "Sorry, our mistake" but that didn't happen. So after we had gone through all the paperwork, I was loaded onto the sweatbox. "OK," I thought, "Cat C, here I come!"

When I arrived at Buckley Hall, the first thing I noticed was that there was no wall. It was just a large fence with razor wire running around the whole perimeter. The second thing I noticed was that it seemed to be surrounded by hills. The prison is in Rochdale, on the edge of the Peak District, sitting on top of Bleak Hill.

I was let out of the sweatbox, and walked into reception. I'm not sure how long I was there, but while I was waiting a lady came to see me. She wasn't wearing a uniform, so I knew she wasn't a screw.

"I'm Rita," she said, pleasantly. "One of the chaplains. Are you Darrell?" I was wondering how she knew who I was when I got my answer: "The chaplain from HMP Wolds has called us to say you were coming, and to watch out for you." I knew from that point on that things were going to be very different here.

The lady was called Rita Nightingale, and it turned out that she had a similar tale to tell of how God had turned her life around. Rita, a man called David Hirst (the Church of England chaplain) and a lady named

Joyce Mulvee formed part of the chaplaincy team at Buckley Hall, and would become a great influence and help in my life. I settled into my new prison, and quickly became part of life at the chapel. They had an Alpha course here too, so I went along for a second time, and found out that you always seem to discover something new on Alpha, no matter how many times you attend. I was also attending Bible study groups and prayer meetings; anything and everything I could go to, I did. I was given my first Study Bible, and I would sit in my cell during bang-up and read entire books at a time. It was all completely new to me and I just couldn't get enough. The Bible, to me, was like an instruction manual for life, and it gave me more information about who God is, how He felt about me, and how He wanted me to live.

I was a popular kind of guy and swiftly got to know a lot of people. Some of the inmates knew me by my old reputation, but most of them were seeing the new me without any of the baggage from my old life. There was one old con who simply could not get his head around the massive change in me. "You used to be a good lad when you were a criminal," he moaned. "I understand criminals, but I don't get all this God business!"

CHAPTER 10

SO FREE

I was growing more and more into the person God had always intended me to be. I used to think a reputation made you a big man but I had more respect from people now than I had ever had in my old life.

The prison was broken up into wings A through to F. I was initially put on D wing, but the prison had a drug-free unit so I opted to go on there. You were tested more regularly to prove you were clean, but you also gained more privileges, such as more association time and extra visits. I ended up with a job as the chapel orderly. This was great because it meant I got to spend every day there and I could chat about God and all the things that I was learning.

One day, we were having a prayer time with just me and some of the other inmates. I had been reading the book of Acts in the Bible and learning about what happened when the disciples were filled with the Holy Spirit. I knew I had been forgiven and I knew God had touched my life because of what had happened in my cell, but I still felt like God wanted to give me more. As we were praying, something strange started to happen. I had this overwhelming feeling of heat running through my body. It went on and on. The other lads with me were feeling the same way too. Then we all started to laugh hysterically. It was great! I couldn't explain or rationalize it; I knew very little about what happened when God filled you with His Holy Spirit, but I knew for sure it was Him.

The next day I was in the chapel talking through what had happened in the prayer meeting. We looked at Scripture and talked about who the Holy Spirit is – God is Trinity, three but one, Father, Son (Jesus) and Holy Spirit. We talked about praying in "tongues", how it is a gift from God and one of the first signs that somebody is filled with the Holy Spirit. We looked at how the gift can manifest as someone passing on a message from God in a language that they have never learned. We also looked at how it can be a "heavenly" language that allows you to express your feelings to God when you just don't know what to say. It all sounded amazing and fantastic to me, and I wanted some of it.

That night after bang-up, I knelt by my bed and began to pray. I'm not sure how long I was praying for, but after a while I began to pray in tongues! It freaked me right out, so I stopped and went to bed. The next day I told Rita and Joyce. They told me to pray again.

"And this time," they said, "just allow God to do what He wants to do."

That night, I gave it a go. I knelt down again and began to pray. Almost straight away I began to pray in tongues, but I stopped trying to fight it and just let it happen.

I honestly had no idea how long I had been there; I lost all sense of time. But it wasn't until I heard the screws banging the gates that I realized ... It was the next morning!

Life had never been so good. I had bars on my window but I had never felt so free. I wanted everyone I knew to find what I had found. We were still doing Alpha, but by now I was helping to run the course. It was 1999; I had been at Buckley Hall for a while and was working towards my release date of August 2000, but it wasn't something that was occupying my mind as I was having a great time in prison!

More and more people were becoming Christians, and the numbers at the Sunday service kept going up and up. I knew that food would bring people out of their cells and into church, so we asked one of the governors if we could serve brunch after the service on a Sunday. Every Sunday morning we would get a fry-up for breakfast; it was one of the highlights of the week. I knew that if we could serve brunch but with bigger portions, then people would come to church just for the food. They would skip breakfast on the wing and come to the chapel because it meant bigger portions after the service! And they did. We were packing the chapel out, and we got a chance to talk to people over brunch afterwards and invite them to Alpha, Bible study, and prayer groups.

Every person in the prison had issues they were dealing with, and I found myself becoming the unofficial prison counsellor. I would be walking around the exercise yard giving advice or just being a listening ear to one person after another. The whole time they were talking I was silently praying, "God, any moment now this guy is going to shut up and he'll want me to say something that will help him. I don't know what to say, so as soon as I open my mouth will You please give me the words?" And He did, every time without fail.

As we continued to help people, more and more of them were becoming Christians, but the same issue would come up over and over again ... drugs. Everyone had either been an addict or still was one. I knew something needed to be done, but I wasn't sure what.

One of the guys in there who had also become a Christian was called Tommy. Tommy had been an addict who had been given twelve years for intent to supply Greater Manchester. He wanted to take what he knew about drugs and addiction to use it and make a difference in someone else's life. I wanted to do the same and the Re-Think project was born. With a flip-chart pad and some markers we designed a course that would help people understand their addiction and find a way of being set free just like we had. It was a success, and the prison governors, health centre staff and education department based in the prison got behind what we were doing. More and more people were choosing to live a drug-free life, and through friendships they came to know God just like we had. The prison had to turn another wing into a drug-free unit to cater for everyone! Later, when I came out of prison, I felt a clear pull from God to help prevent young people from falling into drugs. I changed the Re-Think project to become an educational programme, and began by approaching one secondary school; before long, every secondary school in the borough had the Re-Think project. We even won a national award from DrugScope for our work. The project still runs today from my church, Hope Corner Community Church. We have also trained NHS staff, Addaction and magistrates, and officers from Cheshire, Merseyside, Hampshire, the Met and Greater Manchester police forces. It still tickles me that once the police were chasing me for crimes, and now they are chasing me for help. God is amazing.

We continued to look for new ways to reach out to people and let them know that God loved them and wanted to give them a second chance. Christmas is probably the worst time for anyone in prison. It's the time when the separation from your loved ones hits you the hardest. We wanted to do something that would help strengthen and even restore families, so we came up with the idea of a grotto. Loads of churches got behind us from in and around Rochdale. They went out and purchased hundreds of really good presents and sent them all in. We got permission from the governors to turn one of the private areas usually used for solicitors' visits into a grotto, and we even managed to get the governors and probation officers to take it in turns to dress up as Santa! Over that Christmas period every dad whose children visited was able to take them into the grotto, give them a gift, and have a Polaroid picture taken with their kids. It was so simple, but every man knew that it was the Church that had done this, and it was all because we wanted them to know that God cared about them. Christmas was still a hard time, but that year it was a little easier for all those men and their families.

Things were going really well until I was given some news that really shook me. It was after evening roll call, so we had all been locked up and I was settling down for another night in my cell, when the observation flap opened and someone tapped on my door. It was one of the night staff.

"We've had a phone call from your dad. Your granddad's in hospital. Your dad says he's dying."

"What!" I'd known that my granddad wasn't well, but I didn't think that it was so serious. "Can I use my phone card?" I asked.

"Not until you're opened up tomorrow." With that, he shut the flap. Most of the prison officers in there were great, but this one had just dropped a bombshell and left! I didn't know what to do, so I just sat there and prayed. The next morning they opened me up and I got on the phone. My dad said he had asked if I would be able to have day release to see my granddad as we were very close, but they had told him no because Granddad wasn't classed as immediate family.

I felt useless, cut off. The family hadn't even told my granddad that I'd gone to prison – it would have broken his heart. I went to the chapel and we all prayed together that God would intervene, and that I would get to see my granddad before he died.

That night there was another surprise. Two prison officers opened my door after bang-up. "The governor has given you permission to see your granddad tomorrow," they said. "Two officers will escort you and you'll be in custody cuffs."

"Yes!"

God had come through again! To this day I don't know what He did to change the governor's mind, but He did it somehow. They were paying for a taxi from Rochdale to the cardiac hospital in Leeds and two officers to escort me all the way. I thanked God that night. I was quickly learning that there is nothing He cannot do.

The next day we went down to reception, and I was cuffed to each officer, one on either side. We got in the taxi, and away we went. When we arrived at the hospital, we went to the reception area, asked which ward Eric Tunningley was on, and went to the lift.

The lift doors opened. There were five or six people already in it. They took one look at me and, as if they had rehearsed it, they all took one step back. It took a second to register what had just happened. But then I saw it from their point of view. The doors had opened and there stood a 6ft 2in bloke with a shaved head, handcuffed to two prison officers! I chuckled to myself and we stepped in.

I had been told that I would be cuffed at all times, but as we were about to go onto the ward the two officers stopped me. "We don't want your granddad to see you like this, eh?" And they took the cuffs off and let me go in on my own. My family were around the bed, and I got to sit with my granddad, and pray for him. He had a mask on, forcing air into his lungs to stop them filling with fluid, and he had a line directly into his heart pumping drugs in. He couldn't really talk, but he was definitely trying to say something; I finally figured out that he was asking for a cup of tea – he loved his tea.

I went to the nurse. "Can he have a cup of tea?"

She shook her head. "We can't remove the mask."

"Is he going to live much longer?" I asked.

"No."

"Well, then," I said, "please let him have a cup of tea."

She checked with the doctor, and he allowed it. That was the last thing I got to do for my granddad – he had his cup of tea. That night my granddad passed away. I don't know for certain that he heard my prayer or found God, but I don't believe God would have gone to all that trouble for nothing.

CHAPTER 11

A NEW DIRECTION

One of the best things about being in prison as a Christian is that you can live for God and say more by your actions than you can with your words.

We Christians would get together at association time and have Bible study and prayer groups in each other's cells – I suppose we were the original cell church! – and everyone would notice. The Bible describes this kind of living as being a light in the darkness (see the Gospel of Matthew, chapter 5, verses 14–16), and that was really how it felt. The first Christians were called "People of the Way" because the way they lived was so different from everyone else around them; and that's what we were experiencing. When you're surrounded by so much darkness and pain it just makes it easier to shine, to stand out and be different.

Living like this meant we often stirred people up and got them thinking about their own lives without really having to say anything to them.

There was a lad on my wing called Robbie. He lived a few cells down from me and we had talked a few times but he always insisted that he didn't believe in any of "this God stuff". One Saturday afternoon we were on association time on the wing. All the cell doors were open during association, so you could go pretty much wherever you pleased. I was sitting in my cell reading my Bible, when I heard the squeak of Reebok trainers coming down the landing on the metal checker-plate floor. Out of the corner of my eye, I noticed somebody walk past, and then I heard the trainers squeal as the person turned around and walked back. Robbie was standing at my cell door.

"All right. What's up?" I said.

"I want what you've got."

"Eh?" I had my Bible in my hand so I said, "What, this?"

"No." He shook his head. "I want what you've got in here – you're always happy, and calm. The screws stay off your back. They even come to you for advice. I'm not sure what it is you've got, but I want it. But I don't want any of that God business!"

I knew I had to choose what I said next very carefully. "Well," I said, slowly, "you've got two problems. Firstly, what I've got isn't mine to give you. And secondly, it can only come from God."

He came into my cell, put the seat down on the loo and sat on it. We talked for a while, and guess what? Robbie asked Jesus into his life right there, sitting on my toilet.

Those really were great days for me. We were allowed to have a large room in the health-care unit which we used for prayer meetings; we'd have three-hour prayer meetings in that place, and on one occasion the Holy Spirit hit every single one of us. We were rolling on the floor laughing; we were just on fire. It was awesome.

I was twenty years old, and I had made a deal with God that my life was His. I knew that I would never be a "submarine Christian", surfacing on a Sunday and submerging for the rest of the week. I knew I had to live all-out for Him, and to me that meant full-time ministry. I know that all Christians are, in a sense, in "full-time" work for the Lord. But for me, I knew it would mean going into the ministry.

One of the chaplaincy team was a Methodist minister named Malcolm Bailey. We had spent a lot of time talking about me being a minister – and he also taught me how to play guitar. He pointed me towards a place called Cliff College. It was a Bible college where you could train to be a minister. It sounded right to me, and I wanted to know more. Malcolm arranged for me to have day release from prison so I could go for an interview. The request was granted, and my dad agreed to pick me up from the prison to take me.

When we arrived at Cliff College, I thought the building looked like a huge stately home. I was shown around, and then I had an interview with the principal. We talked and I shared my story. Then he asked how I would cope financially, so I said, "If God wants me to be here, He will sort that out."

"That's good enough for me," he replied. He offered me a place, and I thought that would be it for me – this was God's plan. Well, I would become a minister, but God had a different idea about how that would happen. Because unknown to me, while all this was happening, God had already set the wheels in motion that would take me in a direction I wasn't expecting.

One of the guys who had become a Christian in Buckley Hall had been getting visits from his ex-wife. She attended an Assemblies of God Pentecostal church in Runcorn, Cheshire, and she'd been telling them about the things that were happening and all that God was doing in Buckley Hall prison.

By now it was Easter, and we were putting on a passion play, telling the story of the crucifixion. Nothing like this had been done in the prison before. We had permission for two performances over two nights. The first would be for the inmates and prison staff; the second would be for families and friends of the guys who were in the play. We transformed the chapel. The woodwork department built a stage with a huge cross that could be winched up on pulleys as the centrepiece. The local churches loaned us costumes and lighting, then after a few weeks' practice we were all set.

The first night was packed, with over 300 inmates crammed into the chapel. I was playing the part of Jesus – wearing a loincloth – and that meant balancing on a little footplate with my arms tied to the cross while being winched twelve feet into the air. It obviously had the desired effect, because the next Alpha course was packed with people who had been to the play.

On the second night, the chapel was full again, this time with families and friends. Everything went smoothly again, apart from the end; the footplate on the cross had worked its way loose. Everyone commented afterwards how I really looked as if I was in pain while on the cross. But I wasn't acting – I'm not that good! My foot had been slowly sliding down the plate; the sole was cut open from top to bottom.

Among the visitors that night was the woman who had been telling her church all about us. She was with her pastor, a guy called Mark Finch. I didn't know that Mark was coming, or what part he would play in God's plan for my life. After the event, I was introduced to him and found out that he was an Assemblies of God minister.

While we were talking, Mark asked if he could come and see me again.

"Great," I said.

Mark's church, Hope Corner Community Church in Runcorn, had been praying that God would send someone to help them reach out to the young people in their town. I had been praying that God would tell me where He wanted me to go and what He wanted me to do when I eventually came out of prison. Looking back now it still makes me smile how God had carefully laid His plan for me, and how His plan was woven into so many other people's lives.

When Mark came back to see me, he brought two other people from the church, Benedict Mwendwa and Les Budhi. He told me about the church and how they were heavily involved in children, youth and school ministries. I talked a little about my life up to now, and it ended with them asking me to pray about coming to Runcorn.

With about six months to go on my sentence, I was offered a move to a Category D or open prison called HMP Sudbury. It was a really tempting offer, but while I was thinking about what to do, I heard that some of the inmates were saying that I was only playing at "this God stuff" so I could get to a Category D prison. As soon as I heard what had been said, I knew what I had to do.

I walked to the wing office. "I don't want my Cat D," I said. "I want to finish off my time here."

They couldn't believe it. They said that nobody had ever turned down a chance of going to a Cat D before. But for me, it was an opportunity to show anyone who doubted that it was Jesus who was calling the shots in my life, and that He meant more to me than a move to an open prison.

By this point I didn't have long left on my sentence, and I had a few options about what to do and where to go when I was released. There were a couple of churches in Rochdale offering me positions as a youth worker; a drugs project wanted me to work for them for a very nice salary; and an organization called the Pais Project had offered me a place with them. My plan was to choose one of these options, do it for a year, and then take my place at Cliff College and become a minister. I knew I needed to seriously pray about this, because I did not want to make the wrong decision.

Mark and the team came to see me a couple more times, bringing me Bible study material and praying with me. All the time I was praying that God would leave just one door open to me so I would know it was the right one. I began to find that every time I prayed, Runcorn would come to my mind. In many ways, this was the least attractive option because it had so many unknowns. But it seemed to be the one that God was leading me to.

Mark came up again and I told him that I felt God calling me to Runcorn. I also said it would be for a year and then I would be away to Bible college. Boy, did I get that bit wrong!

The time for my release had almost arrived I thought I would be walking out with just the clothes on my back and a £90 discharge grant. A couple of days before, a lady had come to see me. She had wanted to know if I had applied for a resettlement grant. I didn't even know there was such a thing, so she helped me fill out the papers and I thought no more of it. I also had to notify the prison of my new address. If you had no fixed abode (or NFA) then it could delay your release, so I gave them the address of Hope Corner Community Church.

I believed God wanted me in Runcorn, and I had decided to go straight there and not back home to West Yorkshire first – although my relationship with my family was now a good one. They had come to visit me every couple of weeks and they had seen the huge change in me. As I considered my release and thought about it, I remembered one of the things that had happened when I first moved to Buckley Hall. At that point I hadn't spoken to my family for over a year. They didn't want to know me because of what I'd done. But when I got to Buckley Hall I'd written a letter, and my dad had come to see me. He'd arrived in the visiting hall and sat down. And as he'd looked at me, he'd said, "I've got my son back." Today, my relationship with my mum and dad has never been better – and they've both come to know Jesus as their Saviour. Isn't God wonderful? I thank Him both for repairing the damage that I did when I was lost in the world of drugs – and for restoring my family.

CHAPTER 12

RELEASED

It was the morning of my release: 4 August 2000. I was twenty-one years old.

I felt strangely emotional that morning; I was happy that I was leaving, but sad at the same time. Since Jesus had turned my life around, things had been amazing, so I knew I would always look back on that time in prison with a smile. Saying goodbye to friends who I had seen grow in God alongside me, staff who had stopped being jailers and had become helpers, and the chaplaincy team who had done so much to help me know Jesus better (especially Rita and Joyce) was difficult.

Anyway, I said my goodbyes and walked to the reception area. When I got there I was given my few possessions and a big surprise – £300 in cash! The lady who had helped me fill the form in had got me the resettlement grant. This would mean I could buy some clothes.

"Thank You, God!" I said, as I was walked out to the gate by one of the governors. When we got there, he stopped me and handed me a videotape.

"What's this?" I asked.

It turned out that it was footage from a documentary that had been made about the Christians in the prison. He thanked me for all I had done and wished me all the best.

It had been almost four years since I had walked down a street as a free man – not just free of prison, but free from my life as an addict. I kept looking over my shoulder, expecting them to shout at me to come back, telling me there had been a mistake.

I had arranged to meet Mark Finch in a car park nearby. It felt very strange to be walking down a road, and when I came to cross it at the bottom of the hill it took me ages. Every car looked to me as if it was doing 100 miles per hour! I knew they weren't, but it still seemed fast to me. Once I actually managed to cross the road, I met up with Mark and he bought me a coffee from McDonald's. Then we set off for Runcorn.

The church had recently bought a little building at the bottom of Church Street in Runcorn's Old Town. I had been given a bedroom in this building. It was downstairs, just behind the office area. Benedict Mwendwa lived upstairs with his wife, Charity. They were missionaries from Africa who were based at the church. After dropping my things off, Mark took me to his house, and I met his wife, Karen, their two sons, Matthew and Timothy, and their sixteen-year-old daughter, Rebekah. I had no idea just how detailed God's plan was for my life, because I didn't have a clue at that time just how important Rebekah would become to me.

I will never forget that first meal at Mark and Karen's. It was lasagne, and it was the best meal I had eaten for years.

It took me a while to adjust to life outside. I remember the first night in my new home – I couldn't get to sleep in my new bed because it was too comfortable. I ended up sleeping on the floor with my pillows. That morning I overslept because we had had a later night than I had been used to. When Mark came into the office I heard his keys clinking as he opened the door. I jumped up thinking it was the screw's keys. It took me a while to realize where I was!

My parole officer had never met me before. She had received a file that had "High Risk Re-Offender" stamped on the front, and as you may imagine, that rather coloured her idea of who I was.

I initially had to report to her every day at 9 a.m., and because of my file she was very strict. To start with she wasn't interested in my explanations of how I had changed. I became really frustrated because I knew God had saved me; I was not the man I used to be, but I felt I had to prove myself all over again. If I hadn't had God in my life and the support of the church, I would have found it very hard to cope with. I could see how many people failed and fell back into re-offending. It is like this: you feel as if you have served your time and want to start over, but the system is set up to constantly remind you of, and continue to punish you for, your past. As I write this, there is a bill in parliament to change the Rehabilitation of Offenders Act. At the moment my convictions will never be "spent" – I will always have to explain my past.

There was a funny incident a few years ago when my criminal records check was due for renewal. I am now the CRB liaisons officer in charge of safeguarding for our church and the charity we run, Kids First, but back then we used the Assemblies of God to run our checks. When my check came back it had a covering letter telling the church to look carefully before choosing to employ me. It's great that they were being so cautious, but by this time I was already an accredited minister with AOG!

In one way I don't mind having to reassure people that I am not Hannibal Lecter, because every time I have to, it is an opportunity to tell my story and show them how amazing God is and how He loves us all. On the other hand, sometimes I'd just like to be the person I am now without the constant reminder of the person I once was.

Anyway, I eventually won my parole officer over, and finished my licence period. I was now truly free from the judicial system.

The church were able to provide me with accommodation and cover living costs for food, but at the time it was still a young church plant and they couldn't afford to pay me a wage. Because I was just out of prison, I was entitled to go on a government initiative called New Deal. They agreed that the church could be my training placement and because of that, we were able to receive some financial help, and I would be able to claim Job Seeker's Allowance. They also agreed to fund me to finish the counselling diploma I had started in prison. Although I was "unwaged" for the first year, I can honestly say that God never allowed me to go without anything I needed. It was a great time of learning to rely on God and live by faith.

My work began by going with Mark into secondary schools. The church had begun a mentoring programme for young people, and this was to be the beginning of my ministry. The head teacher of the school was a Christian and was willing to trust Mark's judgement and allow an ex-convict fresh out of prison into the school to work with the children. They were both taking a step of faith – Mark was a magistrate as well as a pastor and had spent the last few years building this ministry, so both he and the head teacher were putting their reputations on the line for me.

Things went from strength to strength and we were given an entire corner of the school for our work; it was around this time that we started Xcel Youth Ministries. Xcel began as a Friday night youth group and has grown and developed over the years. Today, we have two nights, Xcel (full of worship, teaching, fun and games) and Xcel Chill (the only under-eighteens' alcohol-free bar in the town). Both nights are run by a great team of youth leaders who have grown up and been discipled within the church. Our schools' ministry has grown, too.

My plan to stay in Runcorn for a year was not the plan that God had for me. As my year was coming to an end, Mark and the team offered me the position of youth pastor. I prayed it through and it felt right. I was then put forward for ministerial status with the Assemblies of God, and began my training as a probationary minister. Today I am a minister with the Assemblies of God in Great Britain.

God did not just bless me in my work, however. He had plans for my personal life – plans that I could never have imagined.

Rita, one of the chaplains, had given me some great advice about relationships before I was released from prison. She told me to keep my eyes firmly fixed on God, and let Him bring the person into my life that was right for me. That's exactly what I did.

Mark's daughter Rebekah and I had become good friends, and I cared about her deeply. Then one day, out of the blue, Mark came to see me.

"How do you feel about Rebekah?" he asked.

The question made me think – how *did* I feel? At that point I began to get the sense that she was "the one". Focusing on God allowed Him to bring us together. Being single is a great gift and had allowed me to concentrate on God and all that He had for me. For many people, singleness is where God wants them to stay and there is amazing blessing in that. For me, God had a plan of marriage. He knew I would need someone beside me, and arranged the perfect person to walk with me. We were engaged on 14 July 2004 – I proposed in the gardens beneath the Eiffel Tower in Paris – and we were married on 24 July 2005, surrounded by our families and friends. We now get to focus on God together, sharing our passion for Jesus and walking the path He has laid out for us.

So, since giving my life to Jesus I have dated only one girl – and she is the one I married. I cannot imagine life without her. We have been married for six years now and have a son, an amazing little boy called Benjamin who is nearly three, and a lovely baby girl named Lydia.

As we have developed Hope Corner, we have spent £140,000, turning it into a centre of excellence. We now offer the most excellent facilities with the best projects that can help young people turn their lives around and discover a God who loves them. This has meant that we have grown as a church and grown in influence in the borough. We now have contracts with the council to work with the hardest-to-reach young people. We have also grown nationally, and partner with larger organizations such as Tearfund and Faithworks. We have helped to roll out the Discovery Project for Tearfund, helping churches to start and run sustainable social action projects in their communities. This kind of resource wasn't available when we began our work, so in our case, we had to learn as we grew; but this project allows churches to learn from others and start from a firm foundation.

Through our partnership with Faithworks, we also won the Community Innovation Award in 2006 for our Progressive Social Inclusion Project (or PSI). We were invited to London and received it in Westminster. It was a surreal experience; me, an ex-con, at the Houses of Parliament with my wife, Rebekah, and Mark, and his wife, Karen, receiving an award! When we began our work mentoring young people in schools, the council were very "anti-Church"; the Church as a whole did not have a reputation of professionalism or excellence. God has enabled us to change that view, with the local and national government turning to us for advice and guidance.

I now lead the church alongside Mark and we are continuing to go from strength to strength. My life now is so exciting; God has opened so many doors, and given me so many opportunities – I have travelled to North and South America, all across Europe and to Africa, and it's all because of Jesus.

Hope Community Church's greatest current challenge is growth; not a lack of it, but an explosion – we are now seeing a greater demand for our services than ever before. So we are building a second centre. This will house the growing congregation and also the first ever independent Christian school in Runcorn. We are opening the centre and the school to meet the needs in our town. This £700,000 project is our biggest step of faith to date, but I am sure it will not be our last.

CHAPTER 13

DARE TO DREAM

A couple of years ago I had to sit with a fourteen-year-old boy in hospital while the doctor told him that if he did not stop drinking he wouldn't make sixteen. He carried on drinking and, after two attempts at suicide, he finally succeeded. So many young men and women today think there is no way out, no way to break this whirlwind that is their life, but there is.

All that God has done through me, all the lives that He has allowed me to reach, every person I have had the privilege of leading to Christ began with two retired nuns and a prison chaplain. If you have read this book because you feel that your life is going down the drain, then just stop and *dare to dream what God may have in store for you.* Remember a heroin addict who was convicted for armed robbery. God came into his life and gave him a future that he could never have dreamt of. But don't be impressed by me; I've got nothing to do with it. I made a mess that God sorted out. What impresses me is a young person who chooses to live for God now instead of taking the easy option like I did – someone who does not choose drugs or drink but stands up and goes against the flow, then lives an amazing life, achieving more than I ever could. I tell all the young people that I disciple that my ceiling is their floor; however high I may reach in God, that is their starting point. Why do I tell them that? So they will reach far higher than I have, or will.

If you're reading this wondering how you can reach out to people like I do, just start a conversation. Maybe you're telling yourself you're too old, too different from the youth you see around you, that you don't have anything to offer. But just like those old nuns who sat in a room full of convicts, you have all the answers they need. You know the only Person who can turn their lives around; you have the only solution to their problems. You can introduce them to Jesus. God has given you all you need to reach out to them; you just have to start a conversation. Remember that God gave you two eyes, two ears, two hands and two feet, but only one mouth. We should see twice as much, listen twice as much, do twice as much, and go twice as far before we ever speak. I believe that in modern-day Britain we must earn the right to be listened to by showing the love of God. Once the young people see that love, they will ask the questions that will lead them to Jesus. The great command is to love God and to love those around you; the great commission is to take the good news of what Jesus has done, to everyone. But these two things need to work together. If we are going to show the world that Jesus saves, we first have to demonstrate this salvation in ourselves – and get our hands dirty.

THE STEPS

Before I did the Alpha course, I thought Jesus was a historical figure and a "good man". But I discovered that He is alive. He's my lifeline; I couldn't live without Him. My life wouldn't be the way it is if Jesus wasn't exactly who He claimed to be.

If my story has spoken to you, if you want to do something about your life right now, if you want to find the forgiveness that is on offer to you through Jesus, then you might want to think about following these simple steps.

Step 1: Believe that God loves you, and wants more than anything to have a relationship with you.

Step 2: Admit to God that you have done things wrong and that you are willing to turn away from your old ways of sin, and live a new way, in His power.

Step 3: Believe that Jesus died on a cross for you, for your sins, and He did it to give you eternal life.

Step 4: Knowing that Jesus took the punishment for everything you ever said or did or even thought that was wrong, accept Jesus into your life.

Step 5: Pray. If you do not know what to say at first, you can use this simple prayer as a guide. But don't be afraid to say what is in your heart, because God wants you to be honest with Him.

Dear Jesus,

I need You. I believe that You loved me so much that You gave Your life for me. I believe You are God's Son and that He raised You from the dead so that You could give me a new, clean and eternal life. Thank You for dying on the cross for me and for providing the only way for me to have a relationship with God.

Please forgive me for all the things I have done wrong. Come and live in my heart now, and fill me with Your Holy Spirit so that I can live for You by Your own power. Please be the Lord of my life. Teach me how to love You and walk with You every day.

I pray this in Jesus' name. Amen.

Step 6: Tell someone what you have just done. Find someone who knows Jesus too – a youth pastor, church leader, or one of your friends who know Him. Ask them what to do next, and how you can start to live the amazing life that God has for you. (If you don't know anyone, ask the person who gave you this book. Or contact me on the email address below.)

CONTACT

If you would like more details about our work at Hope Corner Community Church, would like some advice or training, or would like me to come and share my story, then please visit www.hopecorner.co.uk for details of how to get in touch. Or email me at darrell@hopecorner.co.uk.

ABOUT THE AUTHOR

After a life of crime and drug addiction, Darrell Tunningley found himself in prison for armed robbery. But while in HMP Wolds, Darrell attended an Alpha course and God broke through into his life. From that day on, Darrell has lived for Jesus and uses his powerful testimony to reach those who think they are unreachable, and to inspire the Church. Darrell, now a minister with the Assemblies of God, joined Hope Corner Community Church in August 2000 and is now part of the senior leadership. He is responsible for running Xcel Youth Ministries and The Progressive Social Inclusion Project (PSI), the award-winning and highly successful social action project, working with excluded and marginalized young men and women in Halton. He is married to his beautiful wife Rebekah, and has two children: a little boy named Benjamin and a little girl, Lydia.